# *Hartlepool Memories*

*The publishers would like to thank the following companies for their support in the production of this book*

Main Sponsor
Corus Tubes

Graythorpe Forge & Engineering Ltd

Greylin Engineering Ltd

Hartlepool Water

F.Shotton Ltd

Tilly Bailey & Irvine

W A Smith Insurance Brokers Limited

Yuill Homes

First published in Great Britain by True North Books Limited
England HX3 6AE
01422 344344



ISBN 1 903204 98 4

*Text, design and origination by True North Books*
*Printed and bound by The Amadeus Press*

# Hartlepool Memories

# CONTENTS

# INTRODUCTION

Welcome to 'Hartlepool Memories', a book which celebrates, and reflects on, how life has changed from late Victorian times to the 1960s when town centre redevelopment altered the face of our town. The images on these pages, accompanied by thought-provoking captions give everyone the opportunity to see how things once were. Many coastal towns claim that they were once parts of submerged kingdoms, but our town can actually show some evidence. At low tide, it is possible to walk across terrain that still contains prehistoric tree stumps and, if you have a keen eye, it is possible to spot a few flints deposited by inhabitants 7,000 years ago. In the early 19th century well-preserved trees and deer antlers were discovered under the surface of The Slake, the marshy area near the headland. The old Anglo Saxon for the area was Heret eu or Stag Island. The headland area, or Heugh, is where the old town is located. St Aidan founded a monastery here in the 7th century for both men and women, though this was destroyed by the Danes 200 years later. St Hilda's Church, named for the monastery's second abbess, now occupies the site. It was erected in the 13th century to provide a resting place for the remains of the De Brus family, local Norman landowners. Hartlepool's strategic position on England's northeast coast meant that it was threatened from both the sea and from land. Some of the medieval town walls built to defend the town, including the historic Sandwell Gate, can still be seen. Hartlepool became an important port during this era, but its influence gradually declined until the harbour fell into disrepair in the early 19th century. However, the sea continued providing locals with a livelihood through fishing. No book on Hartlepool would be complete without mention of the famous monkey. This event from the time of the Napoleonic Wars was popularised by the Victorian music hall entertainer Ned Corvan; soon everybody knew the story. The town has turned what might have been an embarrassing tale into one of pride and humour. This was never more evident than in 2002 when Stuart Drummond, the soccer team's mascot, H'Angus the Monkey, was elected the town's mayor. So happy are we to have the story celebrated of the hanging as a spy of the poor animal washed overboard from a French ship, that images of the creature now adorn promenade walks and club badges. The population of Old Hartlepool was less than 1,000. Change rapidly occurred with the industrial revolution. The West Hartlepool Dock Company helped generate a new town, which within half a century had twice the population of its older rival. The West Hartlepool Rolling Mill, later the West Hartlepool Iron and Steel Company, produced iron plates for shipbuilding; sadly heavy industries declined, and the last shipyard closed in 1962. The two Hartlepools merged in 1966. But now it's time to begin turning the pages and relive the more recent times through which our parents and grandparents lived. There will be events, buildings and faces that even we can bring back to mind with the assistance of the images and text. Once again the cobles will go out into the North Sea, the bombers fly overhead and Father Christmas will turn up at Robinson's department store. Remember when mobile phones didn't disturb the peace? Supermarkets and shopping malls, ugly concrete office blocks and motorways were still to come when the majority of these images were captured. Relive the days when trams ran along Church Street, men offered ladies their seats and shopkeepers still sold cloth by the yard. It is time to recall when grandma danced the jitterbug and grandad was in khaki. Suck on a Spangle or have a sip of dandelion and burdock. Put Neil Sedaka's 'Oh Carol' onto the Dansette record player and let the nostalgia begin!

TEXT ANDREW MITCHELL, STEVE AINSWORTH
PHOTOGRAPH COMPILATION TONY LAX
DESIGNER SEAMUS MOLLOY
BUSINESS DEVELOPMENT EDITOR PETER PREST

# STREET SCENES

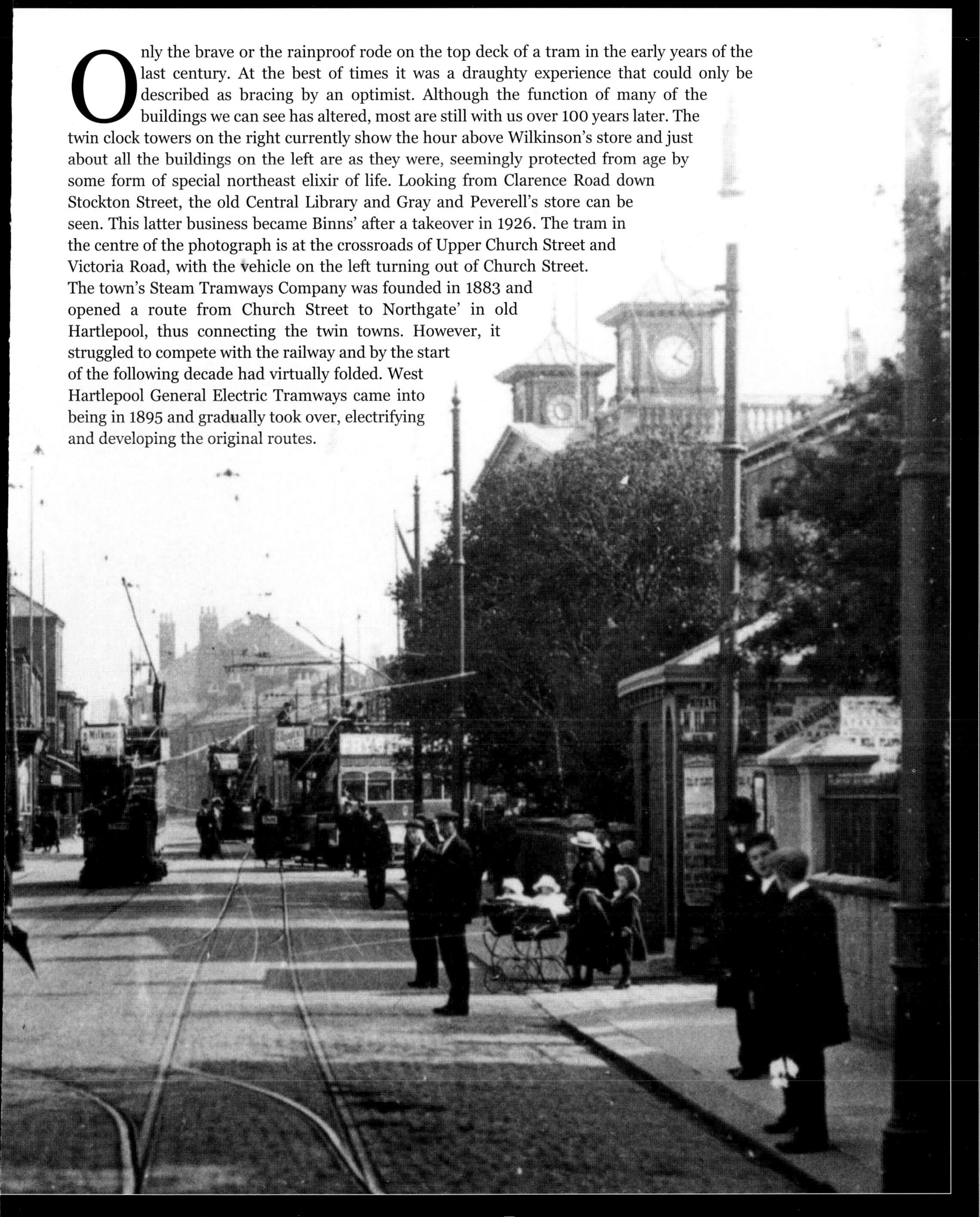

Only the brave or the rainproof rode on the top deck of a tram in the early years of the last century. At the best of times it was a draughty experience that could only be described as bracing by an optimist. Although the function of many of the buildings we can see has altered, most are still with us over 100 years later. The twin clock towers on the right currently show the hour above Wilkinson's store and just about all the buildings on the left are as they were, seemingly protected from age by some form of special northeast elixir of life. Looking from Clarence Road down Stockton Street, the old Central Library and Gray and Peverell's store can be seen. This latter business became Binns' after a takeover in 1926. The tram in the centre of the photograph is at the crossroads of Upper Church Street and Victoria Road, with the vehicle on the left turning out of Church Street. The town's Steam Tramways Company was founded in 1883 and opened a route from Church Street to Northgate' in old Hartlepool, thus connecting the twin towns. However, it struggled to compete with the railway and by the start of the following decade had virtually folded. West Hartlepool General Electric Tramways came into being in 1895 and gradually took over, electrifying and developing the original routes.

**Above:** Looking along Church Street towards the junction with Stockton Street, across which the distinctive Christ Church stands, this photograph highlights life just before the First World War. The gloriously ornate standards that carried the cables for the tramcars are a delightful testament to the workmanship of our late-Victorian forefathers. The vehicle in the foreground was one of the 16-19 series with a Brill chassis and bodywork by ER and TCW. To the right, we can see the corner of the Yorkshire Penny Bank. This is one of the north's best known financial institutions. It was founded in Halifax in 1859 by Colonel Edward Akroyd and, at its peak, had some 900 branches. It was originally called the West Riding Penny Savings Bank and was intended to be a provident society and form of co-operative. However, it opened as a savings bank, registered under the Friendly Societies Act, with initial deposits restricted to just £30 per annum. In this way, it was hoped to attract smaller investors rather than corporate ones to its non profit making ideals. A year after opening, the name changed to the Yorkshire Penny Bank and sub branches were even opened in schools and church halls as business boomed. The 'penny' was dropped from its name to mark the centenary in 1959, but as the Yorkshire Bank it is still a major force in the banking world today.

pouring. Many of the houses were damp and this, allied to cramped living conditions, meant that respiratory illness was a frequent visitor. Prime Minister David Lloyd George made a promise to the nation at the end of World War I. The government was going to build a land fit for heroes. Those naïve enough to believe such empty commitments waited in vain. Eventually, local initiatives saw the eradication of the worst slums, but by then Lloyd George had disappeared over the political horizon.

**Left:** Housewife's Lane, Seaton Carew, around 1890 was tucked away from the sea front where visitors could promenade quite happily, enjoying the sea air. Pretty little stucco houses were built there and around the Green in the early 1800s, but it was a less attractive spot to raise a family if you lived in the heart of the village. In the 19th century, Britain became the world's first industrial society, but this did not have a great effect on the plight of those living in fishing villages. If they wished to benefit from working in factories and heavy industries, they had to move from the homes where they had been born and bred. There was work in the shipyards, but not for everybody, and villagers often continued to eke out a living from their traditional pursuits of fishing, cockling and collecting sea coal. This mother looked suspiciously at the camera. What would the next century hold for her, we wonder? She was used to a life of hard work and near poverty, for that was the lot of the working classes. They existed from day to day and from hand to mouth, just hoping to get through. Her aspirations for her own family were quite humble. She just wanted her children to grow up healthy and be able to help her in her advancing years.

**Left:** Hip, hip, hooray, but for what reason? We can only guess at the stimulus for this little pet's celebration. Perhaps she was just posing for the camera on Temperance Street in the Silver Street area in 1922. The cobbled streets and worn-out housing were typical of the time. People living here had few of the amenities that we take for granted today. Toilets would have been in the back yard and it was a hardy soul who ventured out there to spend a penny on a cold and frosty winter's evening. Bathtime was conducted in front of the fire in the living room. The old tin bath was dragged in from outside and filled from kettles of hot water. Members of the family used to take it in turns to have a dip and often used the same water, occasionally topped up by another

Traffic on one side of a motorway is often reduced to a crawl as drivers slow down to get a better look at the carnage created by an accident on the other side of the crash barrier. Let us spare a thought for any victims of this bus crash. It must have been a terrifying moment as the large vehicle ploughed through the railings and gradually toppled over on its side. At least Binns still got its advert. The fleet of Corporation buses was once plastered with stickers boasting of the quality of shopping at one of the north-east's major department store chains. It had its roots in Sunderland, where George Binns opened a small drapery in 1807. His descendants expanded the business and established further outlets there and in neighbouring towns. By the early days of the 20th century its array of London and Paris fashions and elegant costumes had attracted such a reputation for excellence that the company became like Topsy as it just 'growed and growed'.

**Above:** The Port Clarence bus had come to grief when it crashed off Tees Road. As usual, a group of interested onlookers had gathered. There is something in our nature that makes us have a ghoulish fascination for such disasters, whether major or minor. People even collect to gawp at houses where murders have been committed or drive miles just to observe the remnants of the charred remains a factory fire. Motorists just love to rubberneck at the scene of a car crash.

**Below:** The very first electric tramcar to be seen on the streets of Hartlepool was, not surprisingly, called No 1. With its Milne's four wheel chassis and gleaming bodywork, it attracted huge interest on Northgate on 19 June 1896. The town was at the cutting edge of technology, being one of the first towns anywhere in the country to have an electric system established. Locals were amazed at the ingenuity of engineers who could produce such a marvellous public transport revolution. They were well experienced in rail travel, having been acquainted with steam locomotives for more than half a century, but the power of the railway engine was there to behold. This was something quite different. The electricity that magically hummed through the wires and provided energy for the trams was something quite awe inspiring. It also made local travel in and around the town so much easier. Rail was for going greater distances, but cables were for short hauls and the local populace could say goodbye to Shanks's pony as they hopped on board the cars that ferried them to and from the shops. Youngsters taking in the scene would have so much to look forward to as a real transport revolution was on its way. Before many years had passed, they would remark on the number of motor cars that were starting to appear on the roads and, as young adults, would crane their necks to look at the first aeroplanes flying overhead.

**Left:** Only the ghosts of shoppers past drift along Lynn Street today. There is an occasional piece of litter blowing along the road, like some tumbleweed in an old ghost town in midwest America. Looking at the street today, it is hard to visualise that once it was West Hartlepool's premier shopping area. In 1910, there were so many shoppers out and about that they spilled over onto the street. Sometimes, they were forced there as shopkeepers spread their wares out on the pavement as an added incentive for the Edwardian version of an impulse buyer. Prinskys, on the right, was a popular jewellers. Founded by Solomon Prinsky, whose three sons, Elec, Louis and Abraham, all followed him into the trade, the shop was where some of our grandfathers might have gone to choose granny's engagement ring. The family decided to anglicise the name in the 1930s, changing it to Prinsley. Elsewhere on Lynn Street, there was every type of establishment you could imagine trading happily for a hundred years. In time, you could have gone to the Northern Shop, Woolworths, Hardy's store or Walker's butcher shop. There were several fine drinking holes and so much variety for those who simply wanted to linger on the pavement and indulge in window shopping. Ladies who considered themselves refined took tea in one of the cafes and put the world to rights as they discussed Mrs Pankhurst's latest exploits.

**Below:** Workmen were carrying out road repairs in Bell Street as passers-by went about their own business. Some householders lounged in their doorways looking at the scene, seemingly having little else with which to occupy themselves on this day in the 1940s. It is part of the British psyche to enjoy seeing someone else at work, even in such a seemingly mundane task that was anything but inspirational. Bell Street was one of the typical communities of the time. Many families grew up here and lived their whole lives either in the same house or in the immediate vicinity. Everybody knew everybody else and often helped out in times of need. Children referred to adult neighbours as 'auntie' or 'uncle', which meant that there was a level of friendliness without the over familiarity of just Christian name use that youngsters indulge in today. We have seen many a senior citizen wince when some chirpy tot from down the road calls out 'Hiya, Dot', when 'Hello, Auntie Dorothy' would have been the more usual form of address 60 years ago. Back street communities got together by looking out for one another. If a family had a problem there was always someone on hand, whether a friendly neighbour or close relative, to give moral or financial support. It was not a case of being nosey, it was just being helpful.

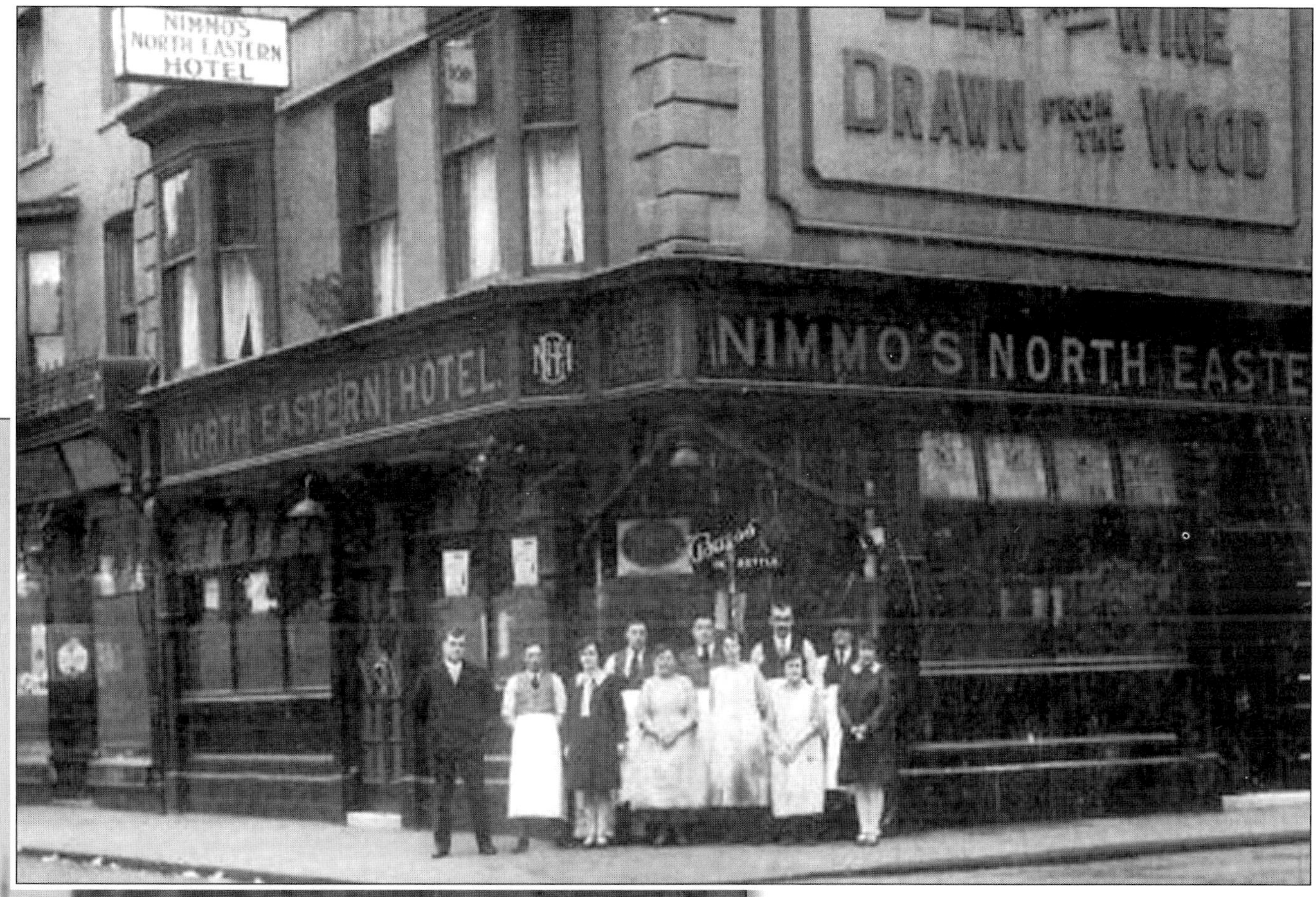

**Above:** What could be better than a pint of real ale drawn from the wood? Who would want anything else, unless it was a glass of wine similarly served from a cask? Before the days when the giants swallowed up the multiplicity of breweries that flourished in Britain, each producer had its own little bit of individuality in the flavour that was dispensed from the pumps or jugs that carried the amber nectar into pint pots. Part of that difference came from the type of yeast, origin of the hops or location of the water used. Some of it was also derived from the nature of the casks in which the liquid was stored. Beer production and supply changed little as the 20th century unfolded, until along came the pressurised canister and the type of ale that was forced up the tubes and emerged characterless. Drinkers from the early 1960s will recall that dreadful apology for beer called Watney's Red Barrel. Like its fellow keg bitters, it was filtered to remove the yeast. It was then pasteurised and carbon dioxide added. By then, any form of acceptable taste had vanished. The beer was forced up from the cellar by more gas and was served, slightly chilled and a little fizzy. Revolting. The staff at Nimmo's North Eastern Hotel, photographed about 1930, would have been horrified.

**Above:** None of these youngsters is with us today as the photograph dates from 1895. Perhaps they did not all make it through the First World War, but let us hope that they did live to a ripe old age. However, that was not a guaranteed matter in late Victorian England. The three score years and ten lifespan was wishful thinking. Such was the high level of infant mortality, life expectancy was just 45 for anyone born a century ago. In deprived areas it was even less as insanitary housing conditions, poor diet, the perils of dangerous occupations and the lack of simple antibiotics and medicines that we now take for granted were major factors. This was the old Croft district on the Headland that was demolished just after the Second World War and here we are looking towards the town walls. The woman on her knees was probably making sure that her front door step was clean and bright. She may have been poor, but she had a sense of pride in the appearance of her home. The first thing that visitors noticed was the condition of the front doorstep, and first impressions are important. We may not remember Victorian England, but many of us will recall our own mothers using a donkey stone as the practice continued well into the middle of the last century.

**Below:** This view of Upper Church Street has changed very little in more than half a century since this photograph was taken in 1950. Access to and from Stockton Street at this junction is now restricted to pedestrians, and although the purpose of the buildings may have changed, the fabric is much as it was. On the immediate left, the first one is now used by the Youth Offending Service, while further along the red brick façade of the Municipal Offices, with its Mare et Industria motto, still imposes itself on the square. The shops on the right may house an optometrist, jeweller and restaurant today, but they are instantly recognisable as the same places pensioners visited in their youth. The former Masonic Hall at the end of the row currently belongs to the College of Art. A small sculpture by the artist Neil Talbot now adorns the centre of the paved area. It was officially received by the Mayor, Gwynneth Hanson, on 15th May 1995. Sharp-eyed readers might just make out the statue of Sir William Gray, who became the first Mayor of West Hartlepool in 1897. It was erected thanks to public subscription in 1898, the year of his death. Behind him, the distinctive Christ Church is now the town's art gallery. Built with money provided by Ralph Ward Jackson, it was consecrated in 1854. However, falling attendances and house clearance in the area saw it hold its final service in 1973.

Thought to have been taken in 1888, this photograph of a Seaton Carew shop shows a group of young lads keenly interested in what might be on offer behind the glass. Unfortunately, we cannot tell too clearly what it was that had attracted them, but it must have been something special to hold their attention. Would it have been bulls' eyes, those sweets that changed colour, or a top and whip to play with in the street? Children made their own amusement as there was no TV, radio, cinema or frippery of electronic gadgets to entertain them. Chasing games, football and making dens kept them busy. On this day, these lads could count themselves among the lucky ones of their generation. So many of their younger siblings perished as infants, succumbing to the sort of diseases that have either been eradicated or controlled by 20th century drugs and improved sanitation. Whooping cough, scarlet fever, measles, influenza and other common ailments were enough to cut a swathe through the young. Life expectancy for a male infant was less than 45 years, though if you managed to survive until the age of these boys there was every hope that you would make it through to your 60s. When this photo was snapped, Seaton Carew had become a holiday resort of some note, rivalling Redcar in popularity.

Croft Gardens as they appeared in 1950, as planting out was nearing completion. The gardens provided a tranquil oasis of space where local people could relax and enjoy a moment or two of peace and quiet in a beautiful setting close to St Hilda's church and the centre of Hartlepool. The gardens took their name from the Croft, an area of land between the market place and the coast which was home to people who made their livings from the sea. The quality of the housing stock here was mixed, and the area had more than its fair share of damp, insanitary dwellings which were removed in the late 1930s. This scene is dominated by the Borough Buildings municipal offices and the much newer semi-detached property housing Verrill's popular fish and chip shop.

VERRILL

**Above:** The Yorkshire Bank building on Church Street, seen in 1970, is still in place today, though the main branch is now on York Road, near the new library. The original Penny Bank was demolished after heavy damage was inflicted on it during the bombing raids of the late summer of 1940. The company was founded in 1859 in Halifax, West Yorkshire, by Colonel Edward Akroyd as a philanthropic organisation aimed at providing a means of saving for the working classes. It was popularly known as Yorkshire Penny Bank, reflecting the interest it had in promoting savings of small amounts by people who only had a modest income or a tiny sum to invest. This was a distinct change in financial attitude as the majority of banking institutions were geared up to deal with the wealthy and showed little regard for the needs of the lower strata of society. It was a gap in the market that the Penny Bank filled noting that, although the working classes may not have had vast sums at their disposal, they existed in huge numbers. Thanks to the rapid expansion of industry, there was a high level of employment rewarded by pay packets, rather than the self sufficiency style of existence that was the norm when the country was largely agricultural in its focus. By 1866 the number of branches reached its peak at 955.

The spectators' clothing at this great fire would need a good soaking with Oxydol to get rid of the grime and flecks of dirt that fell down as the conflagration raged. The soap powder being advertised on the billboard to the right was one of a group of laundry aids that have entered our nostalgic memory banks. Some have stood the test of time, but others have disappeared from the supermarket shelves. We can list Daz, Surf and Tide as some of the major players in this market, but where did Rinso get to? Some travellers might come across this old fashioned name on their holidays, as it is still manufactured in Turkey and the Far East. Yet, what is in a name? Somehow Omo managed to survive. The soap powder industry has given us some of the most memorable, as well as the worst, television adverts. The doorstep challenge has been a familiar thread for almost half a century. With Jimmy Young or Craig Douglas pushing a packet and a microphone under a housewife's nose, the latter had little alternative but to express delight with the product being promoted. Those viewing the flames lighting up the night sky ignored the Oxydol advert and concentrated on the work of the brave firefighters who had just arrived to deal with the warehouse down at the docks that was about to be reduced to just so much rubble.

**Below:** By 1973, as he passed Clarence Road bus station, the rag and bone man had become something of a museum piece, but this one still seemed to be doing good business. At one time his cry was a familiar one on our back streets on a weekly basis. Housewives were invited to bring out their unwanted goods in exchange for a bar of soap, a few pegs or the more usual donkey stone that was ideal for applying to the front doorstep to make it gleam that bit better than those of the neighbours. Sometimes he would appear on the street corner with balloons attached to his cart or bobbing above the horse's mane. Excited children alerted their mothers to his presence in the hope that they would receive a balloon as part of the exchange. Gardeners followed behind with a bucket and shovel hoping for something with which to enrich their rhubarb patch. The totter, as he was known in some areas, collected rags for converting into fabric and bones that could be processed into glue. He was something of a latter day recycling plant. Scrap metal would also be collected and traded or sold on to other merchants. The rag and bone man played a part in society as a very useful component in the days before most of us had motor cars. Householders had limited ability to travel to collection points or rubbish dumps and he serviced a social need.

**Right:** The young mums pushing their prams near York Road in May 1963, in front of the No 6 bus to West View, were enjoying the sunshine of the late spring. It was marvellous to get out in the fresh air, let the warm breeze waft through your hair and enjoy the chance to parade around in short sleeved blouses and lightweight skirts. Only a few months earlier it had been a far different scenario as this had been the winter of the big freeze. Right from the start of the year, the Arctic conditions held the country firmly in an icy grip. Rivers froze over and children built igloos in their back gardens. Power cuts made us even more miserable and, for a while, whole rural communities were marooned and needed the RAF to airlift food parcels to them. Farmers fed livestock via bales of hay dropped from light aircraft and the football season had to be extended in order that the programme could be completed. We even had the quaint sight of a panel of experts meeting up each Saturday to predict the soccer results so that the pools companies could operate. After the freeze came the thaw and its attendant flooding. But, once summer appeared on the horizon, all the gloom and doom was consigned to the memory banks. Out came the pushchairs and buggies and it was off to the park for some family fun.

The single decker 'Leopard' No.12 bus ran from Port Clarence to its terminus at Middlegate. The ECW body used by its Leyland manufacturer on this model was just one of many firms that provided the coachwork over the years. Leopards were built between 1959 and 1982, having replaced the less powerful 'Tiger Cubs'. The Leyland Leopard's major direct competitor throughout most of its life was the AEC Reliance, even though AEC was a subsidiary of Leyland for a large proportion of that time. The Leopard was also used for military purposes and was exported to many countries across the globe. Although largely used as intended, some recipients had the vehicles bodied as pantechnicons and car transporters. It was eventually superseded by the 'Tiger', manufactured 1981-93. Photographed in 1968, the bus had just collected passengers crossing from Middlesbrough on the car transporter bridge. This remarkable piece of engineering is the only working example of its type in England. The travelling compartment is suspended by cables from a carriage that runs along the girders, taking two and a half minutes to cross the Tees. It can take up to nine vehicles at a time and transport several hundred pedestrians 160 feet above the waters of the river below. The bridge even has its place in movie history, being featured in 'Billy Elliott', the story of a young ballet dancer.

# AT LEISURE

Even as early as the late 18th century, Quakers from Darlington and Sunderland, many of them well heeled bankers, made Seaton Carew a popular place to come for a holiday. By the time Queen Victoria was settled on the British throne, bathing machines, based on designs used by pioneering swimmers in Scarborough, appeared on the beach. Gas lighting was introduced along the promenade and a new sea wall was constructed, helping to revitalise the village and turn it into a threat to the position Redcar enjoyed as a major resort on this stretch of coastline. These bathing machines, with their adverts for Beecham's famous pills, were photographed in August 1890. Notice the sailor outfits, so popular at the time, worn by several of the young boys. Three years earlier the West Hartlepool Corporation had indulged in a fierce debate that the machines, segregated for male and female use, were placed too close together for the likes of those with stern views of Victorian modesty. One councillor thought that they should be sited 50 yards apart. Seaton Carew continued to attract holidaymakers well into the next century and its attractions included a new promenade that opened in 1905. In the inter-war years of the 1930s, day trippers enjoyed themselves in George Siddle's fairground and in the kiosks and cafés that abounded here.

**Right:** It was a case of X marks the spot for the boys from Galley's Field School in this photograph taken on the promenade about 1900. They did not have far to walk to get here as the school was on the edge of Town Moor. The promenade was built as a sea defence, but soon became a popular spot for people to meet and stroll as they enjoyed the bracing breezes fluttering in off the North Sea. There were times around the start of the 20th century when it seemed as if all of old Hartlepool was out on the sea front, especially at the weekend. In later years Galley's Field would be mentioned in the biography of one its most famous old boys. Reg Smythe (1917-98), became a shipyard worker after leaving Galley's Field at the age of 14. After various jobs, he ended up at the Daily Mirror, having shown some proficiency in producing art posters and cartoons. It was in 1957 that he produced the first Andy Capp cartoon that was to make his name known across the country and even spawned a musical with songs by north-east's own Alan Price. Smythe (born Smyth) returned to live in Hartlepool for the last 20 or so years of his life.

**Left:** Designed by Milburn's, the West Hartlepool Odeon opened on Raby Street as the Majestic on 27th July 1936, but was soon taken over and renamed. With a seating capacity of over 1,500 it became one of the most popular entertainment centres in town. Seen here in the mid 1960s, a night out at the pictures was still a normal way to spend a Friday evening with a boyfriend or girlfriend. The main attraction on this occasion was a good looking young actor called Richard Harris. Playing opposite Rachel Roberts in 'This Sporting Life', Harris took the role of a young miner who becomes a successful rugby league player, but fails to find contentment in his life. Both stars were nominated for Oscars. The first odeons were amphitheatres in ancient Greece and the name was used on the continent for cinemas in the 1920s. Oscar Deutsch (1893-1941) was born in Birmingham, the son of a Hungarian Jew who ran a scrap metal business. Deutsch opened his first picture house in Dudley in 1928 and soon had a chain of them across the country. The art deco style, common to many of these buildings, made his Odeons quite distinctive and a definite step up from the fleapits that many rivals had become. He pretended that his cinema chain took its name from the acronym for Oscar Deutsch Entertains Our Nation, but this was rather tongue in cheek, but a good marketing ploy nonetheless.

**Above:** When the circus came to town was always a special moment in our lives. For several weeks, posters appeared on walls and in shop windows announcing that Billy Smart, Chipperfield or Bertram Mills would be here for the week. As the days went by, children became eager with anticipation, knowing that there would soon be a grand parade through town that announced the arrival of the animals and performers. There was a carnival atmosphere when the day itself dawned and the parade of elephants led the way down the street. They were accompanied by pretty girls in sequinned leotards performing cartwheels and back flicks. Men on stilts towered high above everyone as lorries drove by with lions and tigers in cages. Jolly clowns rode in a car. Every so often, one of the doors fell off as a mock explosion took place. Most kiddies urged their parents to buy tickets for the show, but there were a couple of softies who would later claim to have been emotionally scarred for life by having a man with a painted face, big, red nose and sticky-out hair squirt water from a flower into their faces. When the big top was being erected on the field, children came along to watch the pegs being hammered home and men hauling on the ropes to lift the giant canvas into place. When show time came along it was the perfect rounding off to the magic of anticipation.

**Below:** The Palace Theatre of Varieties on Mainsforth Terrace, like most others of its type, ran two shows per night, such was the popularity of variety at this time. During its existence the building went under a succession of names. It was originally the New Theatre Royal, then the New Gaiety Theatre. Following its change to the Palace, it became the Gaiety in its final years. The crowd waiting outside the theatre in 1930 was ready for a thoroughly entertaining evening. Although whether you were a singer, comedian, dancer or speciality act might mean some minor alterations to a performance dependent upon the venue, the basic material could remain the same until a theatre was revisited. This meant that an act could be well rehearsed and highly polished, giving patrons a feast of professionalism to enjoy. Shows usually began with a small chorus line of dancing girls who kicked their legs and often did little else. The warm up second spot comedian then came on to try to get the audience in a happy frame of mind, paving the way for the bigger names. Jugglers or animal acts followed and then the second name on the bill closed the first half. After the interval, the girls danced again and eventually, after several more turns, the big name came on for the final spot. Great entertainment and a grand night out.

**Above:** Edwardian fashion demanded long dresses, full tops and large hats. Pictured with a few of their children, this church mothers' group met at Middleton School in 1907. Their garb was mainly formal and almost exclusively dark in hue, with the exception of lighter shades worn by a couple of the more adventurous. This rather stern looking collection of ladies was quite a formidable force. They banded together as overseers of moral standards but also kept a watchful eye out for the needy and less advantaged in society to whom they could lend a hand. Although they concentrated on local issues, these mothers had a steely determination that was to spill over into concerns some of them had over matters of national importance. The burning issue of the day for a growing band of women was the one of suffrage. This included voting rights in political elections that were denied to them. In previous times, the right to vote had a property or income qualification. Women had little that they could call their own and were largely regarded as being in the ownership of their husbands. Emmeline Pankhurst founded the Women's Social and Political Union in 1903 and attracted forceful ladies such as those in the picture to the cause. Aided by daughter Christabel, Emmeline fought hard for women's rights until her death in 1928.

The large group of pensioners, seen around 1925, disembarked from the buses and charabancs that provided the transport for their outing. They belonged to a generation that was one of the first to benefit from a state pension. The 1908 Old Age Pensions Act was the first piece of legislation in Britain to award statutory payment to senior citizens on a non-contributory basis. The first cash was handed out from 1st January of the following year and gave 70-year-olds and over a weekly amount of between two and five shillings (10p and 25p), dependent upon a means test. William Beveridge, the economist who helped shape the welfare state introduced during the Attlee government of the late 1940s, was an adviser to the Liberal government that introduced the old age pension. The Chancellor of the

**Below:** The Great War was the one to end all wars, or so we were told when it was over. The politicians forgot all about that statement 20 years further down the line as we went through it all again. Yet, in the beginning, our boys marched off brightly in the early autumn of 1914 with the words 'back by Christmas' ringing in everyone's ears. The stark reality saw 100,000 slaughtered at Ypres alone before the carol singers had finished their wassailing. It was stalemate in the trenches and countless lives were lost as a few muddy yards were gained, only for the enemy to win them back shortly afterwards. By 1915, when this group was photographed, the grim experiences of wounded men returning from the front were related to a public that was only just beginning to realise that modern warfare was not the jolly adventure romantics had led them to believe. In a way, these soldiers were the lucky ones. They convalesced from their injuries at home and enjoyed meeting up with their families once more as they relaxed on the beach at Seaton Carew. How many, though, of these brave men recovered sufficiently to return to active service and later be laid to rest in some foreign field? In the meantime they could enjoy what time they could with their loved ones.

Exchequer at the time, David Lloyd George, was a supporter of the Act, but the money had to come from somewhere. He raised the level of income tax, introduced a new supertax and instituted a swingeing assault on inherited wealth and profits on the sale of property. In the year that our pictured seniors had their day out the state pension was supplemented by the extension of the National Health Insurance scheme, established in 1911, to provide pensions between ages 65 and 70 for contributors, mainly male manual workers.

**Below:** It is here that the only real remnant of the town wall's gates can be found. Sandwell Gate provides a backcloth to the Fish Sands that attracted families to the water's edge in this 1952 photograph. Allied with the natural barrier formed by the cliffs to the east and south, the old wall helped protect the town from the threat of marauding Scots in medieval times. Fishermen also used to bring their boats ashore here and sell their catches on the sands until the Fish Quay was built in 1880 and trade largely moved there. These sands have another link with Hartlepool history as it was here that the famous monkey legend was born. In the early 1800s, the Napoleonic Wars had British citizens in an uneasy mood. Bonaparte's armies were only a few miles away across the Channel from our south coast and his navy was well able to sail further north and launch attacks from the sea along the east coast. When locals saw a French ship of the Chasse Maree class foundered out to sea, not many tears were shed. The story goes that a pet monkey was washed overboard and became the sole survivor of the wreck. Never having seen a Frenchman or a monkey before, local crofters believed that they had captured a foreign spy. He was summarily tried for treason, convicted and hanged on the spot. Or so legend has it.

They strolled along the prom with an independent air, to slightly amend the old music hall song about the man and the bank at Monte Carlo. Taking the air was still quite the fashionable thing to do in the first few years of the last century as we passed from the Victorian age to that of the Edwardian. The ladies looked resplendent in their ground length dresses and extravagant hats. Some strolled with their beaux, carefully chaperoned by a maiden aunt or some other killjoy. The promenade on the headland was built in 1889 and soon became the place to be seen after church on a Sunday afternoon. The bandstand was presented by Sir Christopher Furness MP and was originally open to the elements, not a wise move on the north-east coast. By the turn of the century, after complaints from a succession of soggy bandsmen, it was enclosed. The bandstand was also used as a changing area for actors performing open air plays on the promenade. Spectators could reserve a seat on the concrete banking for 2d (1p). Latterly, the Council has tried to revive some visitor interest in the Headland by promoting a story trail along there, but only a few people walking dogs can be seen passing the concrete steps today and the bandstand is no more.

**Right:** In the inter-war years, mixed bathing became acceptable and very popular in Britain. During the Victorian and Edwardian eras the sexes were usually kept apart when indulging in such a leisure or sporting activity that necessitated the display of areas of bare flesh. Goodness knows what our ancestors would have thought of topless sunbathing or nudist beaches that are commonplace nowadays. They took the view that frolicking in the water close to a member of the opposite sex was a step on the slippery slope to depravity. However, as attitudes became more liberal, many towns built swimming baths that were open to everyone, though there were still restrictions in force in some places. A number developed open air pools or lidos where there was little in the way of demarcation and, despite the vagaries of the British climate, these were very well patronised. Hartlepool took advantage of its position as a coastal town and built its version near the Heugh where bathers could enjoy the saltwater in the safe shadow of the breakwater. The semi-circular pool opened in 1923 and survived for 30 years until the great storms of 1953, that devastated much of the east coast, swept it away when the breakwater was overwhelmed. The damage was irreparable and the town lost a valuable and much loved amenity.

**Above:** Do not let anyone hear you refer to this as an example of old man's marbles. Aficionados of the game will remind you quite forcibly that one of our national heroes, a certain Sir Francis Drake, was not averse to taking a break from fighting Spaniards by bending his back and using a bit of finger bias. Sending a bowl across the green was good practice for aiming a cannonball at the Armada. Seen in 1946, these men were enjoying a game at Ward Jackson Park. To be able to get out and about in the sunshine after the war, without the worry of listening for an air raid siren, was one of the simple pleasures that they had forgotten about. It was good to get back to normal. The large recreation area covers about 20 acres, or 8 hectares if you want to be modern. It was opened in 1883 and paid for by public subscription and was named to commemorate the founder of West Hartlepool. There are numerous delightful architectural features, so reminiscent of late Victorian and Edwardian times. The Lodge House bandstand, fountain, clock tower and lake make it a most picturesque spot and good enough to be included in the National Register of Historic Parks and Gardens. Now, pass the mat and let us see if we can just lodge this next sphere of lignum vitae alongside the jack.

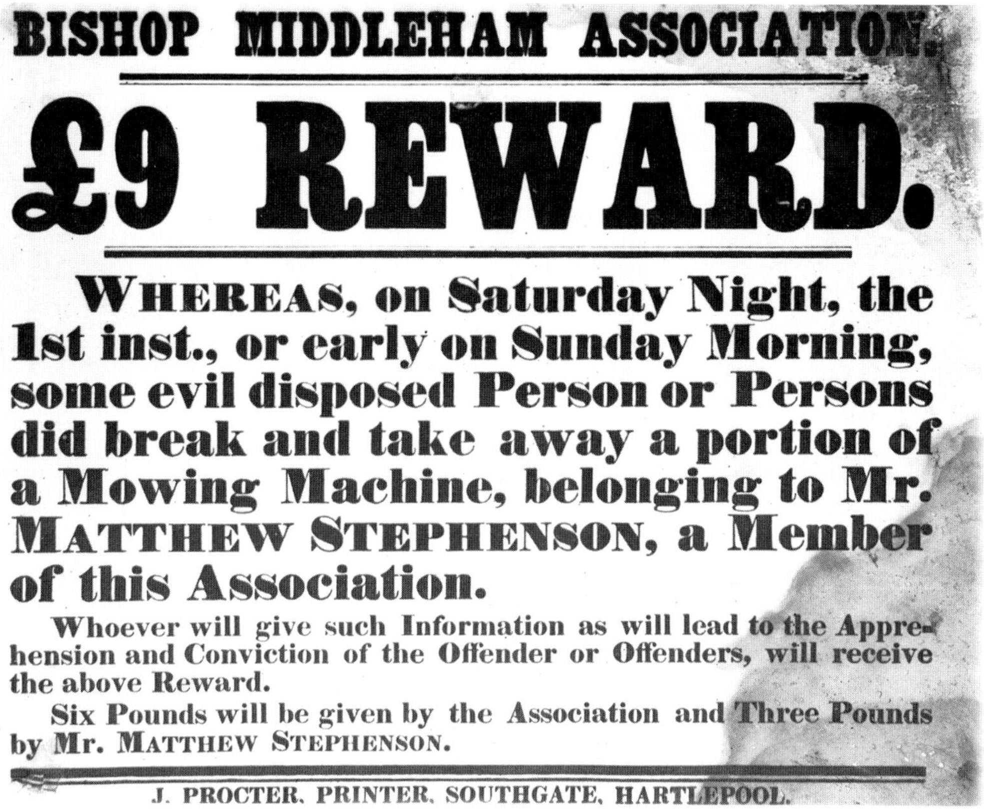

BISHOP MIDDLEHAM ASSOCIATION.

£9 REWARD.

WHEREAS, on Saturday Night, the 1st inst., or early on Sunday Morning, some evil disposed Person or Persons did break and take away a portion of a Mowing Machine, belonging to Mr. MATTHEW STEPHENSON, a Member of this Association.

Whoever will give such Information as will lead to the Apprehension and Conviction of the Offender or Offenders, will receive the above Reward.

Six Pounds will be given by the Association and Three Pounds by Mr. MATTHEW STEPHENSON.

J. PROCTER, PRINTER, SOUTHGATE, HARTLEPOOL.

**Above:** Nine pounds was an awful lot of money when this reward notice was printed. The mowing machine in question was undoubtedly an expensive steam-powered agricultural behemoth used to mow fields not lawns. Our interest in the advert however is primarily focussed on the printer, J Procter, of Southgate, Hartlepool. John Procter ran a printing firm in both Hartlepool and West Hartlepool. He saved a copy of everything he printed, and much of it is now with Hartlepool Museums Services and known as the Robert Wood Collection, after the local historian who saved it. Procter moved to Hartlepool in 1834 to set up business in Southgate in Old Hartlepool. A second printing shop opened in West Hartlepool, in Victoria Terrace, in 1851. Procter did printing jobs for both firms and individuals; he also sold stationery and patent medicines, as well as naval charts. He sold insurance and stamps and booked entertainers, finding them lodging while they were in town. The resourceful printer also ran a book ordering service, sending orders to London for books which were sent north on the next boat. John Procter died in 1860, aged 51. Following his death his wife ran the business until their son, John Kirtley Procter, took over. Following John Kirtley Procter's death in 1884, the firm was taken over by Fred W. Mason and continued on the Headland until Mr Mason's death in 1946. The last printing firm on the Headland, it was then taken over by BT Ord's printing firm, of West Hartlepool.

**Below:** If you want to get ahead, get a hat. This was the slogan that Dunn and Co. adopted in the 1940s. At the

time, most men wore hats of some description, whether it be of the flat, bowler, homburg, trilby or even top variety. Unless you resort to the quaint 21st century fashion style of the controversial Pete Doherty of the Babyshambles pop group, or that of an early Frank Sinatra, it is unlikely that the jauntily placed trilby will make a comeback. By 1968, the hat maker was already seeing trade rapidly diminishing and it began to concentrate on its other lines in men's tailoring. Nearby, the Empire Theatre was one of West Hartlepool's best known buildings. The body of the theatre occupied the length of Freeman Street, though its foyer and entrance were on Lynn Street. After entering, first-time visitors were surprised to find that they had to follow an enclosed passageway that took them across a back street and into the main auditorium. On 13th December 1909, the West Hartlepool Amateur Operatic Society (WHAOS) opened the theatre with a performance of 'The Toreador'. Live theatre struggled to compete with the cinema during the 1930s and 1940s, but the coming of popular television in the 1950s spelt trouble for both media. The Empire closed and reopened three months later on 2nd April 1956 as a cinema. But, it was too late. Trying again a year later as a luxury unit showing 'The King and I' with Deborah Kerr and Yul Brynner made little difference. It reverted to a theatre and one more live show, featuring the return of the WHAOS with 'Carousel', took place on 16th November 1959. The building was demolished in 1975.

**Above:** Saturday night at the Queen's Rink dance hall was a regular entry in any young person's diary during the 50s and 60s. The girls always seemed to go there in twos while the lads turned up in larger groups, often fortified by a swift pint in the Devon beforehand. With such big bands as the Joe Loss Orchestra playing popular tunes, to which we could impress with our nifty fishtail moves in the quickstep or spin turns in the waltz, the Rink was the ideal place to meet a member of the opposite sex. But why did her mate have to be the killjoy and remind her that she had to back home by 11 o'clock? Alternatively, why did his pal think that my friend would find his acne attractive? As the jive replaced the cha-cha, boys with greasy combs in their top pockets whirled around the girls whose starched petticoats billowed out like voluminous tents. When pop groups such as the Hollies or Van Morrison's Them replaced the big bands, the girls moved from the sidelines where they used to sit waiting to be asked to dance. They now held court in the middle of the floor and performed the Twist, the Mashed Potato and the Watusi around their handbags. Unfortunately, this Clarence Road establishment also attracted some unruly elements and it was not uncommon to have to sidestep a group of louts having a punch-up as you tried to make your way home.

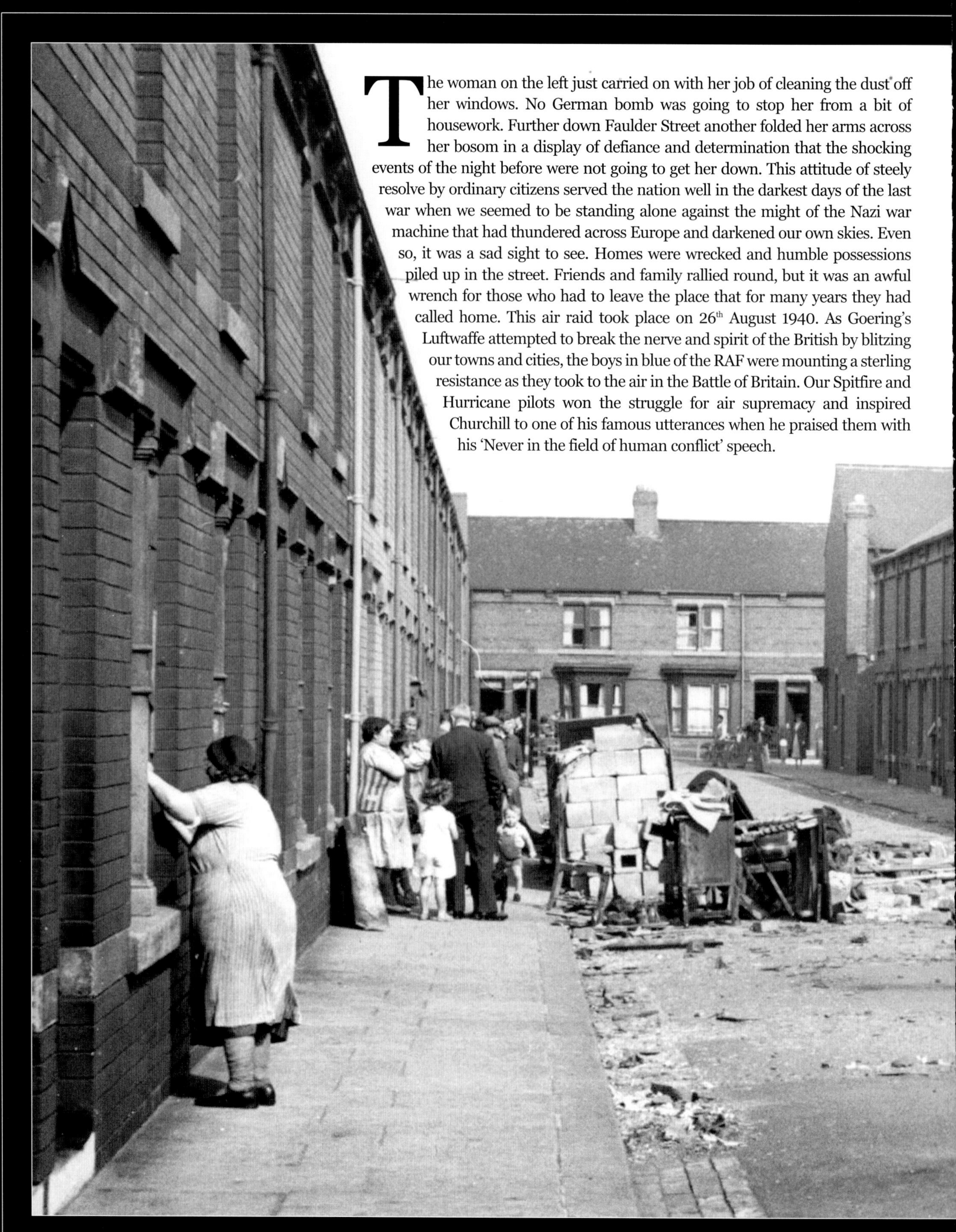

The woman on the left just carried on with her job of cleaning the dust off her windows. No German bomb was going to stop her from a bit of housework. Further down Faulder Street another folded her arms across her bosom in a display of defiance and determination that the shocking events of the night before were not going to get her down. This attitude of steely resolve by ordinary citizens served the nation well in the darkest days of the last war when we seemed to be standing alone against the might of the Nazi war machine that had thundered across Europe and darkened our own skies. Even so, it was a sad sight to see. Homes were wrecked and humble possessions piled up in the street. Friends and family rallied round, but it was an awful wrench for those who had to leave the place that for many years they had called home. This air raid took place on 26th August 1940. As Goering's Luftwaffe attempted to break the nerve and spirit of the British by blitzing our towns and cities, the boys in blue of the RAF were mounting a sterling resistance as they took to the air in the Battle of Britain. Our Spitfire and Hurricane pilots won the struggle for air supremacy and inspired Churchill to one of his famous utterances when he praised them with his 'Never in the field of human conflict' speech.

# WARTIME

Orson Welles panicked America in late 1938 with his realistic radio play that was an adaptation of HG Wells' 'War of the Worlds'. Thousands thought that they were listening to a real Martian invasion. The Hartlepools had witnessed something similar in real life over two decades earlier. This was not a ship from outer space that the searchlights picked out on 27th November 1916, but a German Zeppelin that was part of the enemy war machine. Originally conceived as a passenger airship, the military also recognised its potential as a vehicle that could deliver an effective bombardment on the enemy from the skies. This one zigzagged at 10,000 feet in an attempt to escape the searchlights and the shells aimed at it. In this attack, bombs were dropped on Elwick and West Park, as well as West Hartlepool town centre. Houses were damaged and there were a number of fatalities. Revenge was sweet when the pilot Lieutenant L Pyatt took off from Seaton Carew in his aeroplane and shot at the raider and caused it to burst into flames and crash into the North Sea. This was the second time a Zeppelin had attacked the town, but the previous incident in August 1916 had just damaged a few houses in Longhill. A third raid took place in March 1918 when eight inhabitants lost their lives.

**Below:** In April 1919, the Mayor of West Hartlepool, Councillor TF Thompson, took official receipt of the tank 'Egbert' from Major General EB Swinton in recognition of the town's efforts in a record fundraising enterprise during the 1914-18 war. A mammoth amount had been realised and the presentation took place on Stranton Garth and Egbert was a familiar sight in Vicarage Gardens until 1937. It was one of a number of travelling tanks that had been used up and down the country as towns held Tank Weeks when special drives were held to get locals to invest in war bonds or contribute directly to the war effort. Residents were made to feel as if they had a personal stake in the machine that stood in their town square. Although most of these travelling tanks stayed in Britain and were solely used for advertising purposes, Egbert had seen active service. It was one of those used in the Battle of Cambrai in November 1917 when General Sir Julian Byng was ordered to relieve pressure on the French front. The offensive consisted of an attack against the Germans' Hindenburg line along a 10-mile front. The chosen terrain, rolling chalk downland, was especially suitable for tank movement. Over 300 of these vehicles smashed through German defences and some 7,500 prisoners were taken at low cost in casualties in the first assault.

**Above:** Tank Week began in West Hartlepool on 4th February 1918. 'Nelson' was one of the travelling or presentation tanks of the Lincoln class that toured the country in the latter years of the Great War. When the general public saw Mark IV tanks for the first time during the Lord Mayor's Show in London in November 1917, they was amazed at this new wonder machine. Six of these were sent on tour, like some modern day pop star, spending a week in a town as a sales pitch for war bonds and war savings certificates. Given sturdy sounding names, 'Egbert', 'Old Bill', 'Julian', 'Drake', 'Iron Rations' and 'Nelson', it was the last of these that was put through its paces on the Armoury field and locals from the Hartlepools were invited to try it out for size. War machines and the thinking that underlay them went through a revolution during this war. Military leaders, most of whom were born in the middle of the previous century, had been brought up in the era of the horse and cart. Their strategy on the field at the beginning of the First World War was still linked to cavalry charges and lines of advancing foot soldiers. By the time hostilities ceased, it was the aeroplane and the tank that led the way, providing a blueprint for the second world war 21 years later.

**Below:** Taking the air along the headland at the Heugh, a walker will come across this memorial plaque that reminds the world of the day that enemy action returned to English shores for the first time to any major degree in over 150 years. We had been attacked and invaded before, by various tribes and races from the Romans to the Vikings, from the Normans to the Scots. However, there had been peace on our soil ever since Bonnie Prince Charlie had been sent packing 'like a bird on the wing' and off to the Inner Hebrides. Napoleon threatened to invade, but never made it, and although America's John Paul Jones mounted a minor raid on Whitehaven, it was hardly an incident that threatened national security. So the locals in the Hartlepools gave little thought to war appearing on their own doorstep. They were well aware that the British Expeditionary Force had gone to France in the autumn of 1914, but our boys would be back by Christmas, or so they thought. To be suddenly confronted by German shells whistling through the air and crashing into the town on that Wednesday morning in mid December was a shock to the system. The granite memorial was made in the 1970s by Henry Nicholls, replacing an earlier one that stood there. The plaque was restored in the early 2000s by Carl Paylor.

**Right:** We know quite a lot about women's work during the world wars of the 20th century, but the major portion relates to the 1939-45 conflict. We have read articles or seen documentaries about land girls, ATS women, the WVS, ambulance drivers and those behind the wheel of buses, but it was in the 1914-18 war that we first turned to the so-called weaker sex for assistance on the home front. With thousands of troops heading off into Europe on a daily basis, the wheels of industry and agriculture had to be kept turning. Women went out into the fields with pitchforks to toss the hay and sat astride newfangled tractors to plough the fields and bring in the harvest. They also went into the factories and engineering companies to work on the assembly lines and help build the war machines that were needed at the front. Perhaps the most dangerous of tasks were those undertaken by the girls who went to work in the munitions industry. Surrounded by volatile high explosives, they produced bullets for the soldiers' Lee Enfields, ammunition for 15 inch howitzers, cannon shells for 18 pounder field guns and enough ordnance for the mortars to keep the enemy occupied throughout any number of attacks. It was gruelling work. Although assisted by hoists and other lifting tackle, it was still a backbreaking job for these women to perform. They also lived with the constant fear that a stray spark could cause havoc.



**Top right:** During World War II all sorts of essential and non-essential foods were rationed, as well as clothing, furniture and petrol. Before the conflict started Britain imported about 55 million tons of food a year from other countries. After war was declared in September 1939, the British government had to cut down on the amount of food it brought in from abroad and decided to introduce a system of rationing. People were encouraged to provide their own food at home. The 'Dig for Victory' campaign started in October 1939 and called for every man and woman to keep an allotment. Lawns and flower-beds were turned into vegetable gardens. Chickens, rabbits, goats and pigs were reared in town parks and gardens. Ration Books were issued to make sure everybody got a fair share. This contained coupons that had to be handed to the shopkeepers every time rationed goods were bought. Food was the first to be rationed. On 8th January 1940, bacon, butter and sugar were rationed. It wasn't just food that was limited during World War II. Clothing rationing began on June 1st, 1941, two years after food restrictions started. There was a shortage of materials to make clothes. People were also urged to 'Make do and mend' so that clothing factories and

workers could be used to make items, such as parachutes and uniforms, needed in the battle against Germany. Every item of clothing was given a value in coupons. Each person was given 66 coupons to last them a year. Later it was reduced to 48 coupons. Children were allocated an extra 10 clothing coupons above the standard ration to allow for growing out of clothes during a year. This did not prevent children having to wear 'hand me downs' from older brothers and sisters. In a make do and mend environment, trousers and skirts were patched and darned, old jumpers were unpicked and the wool used to make new garments. Rationing continued even after the war ended. Fourteen years of food shortages in Britain ended at midnight on 4th July 1954, when restrictions on the sale and purchase of meat and bacon were lifted.

How to use this book

1. This Clothing Book must be detached immediately from the Food Ration Book (see page I); and the holder's name, full postal address and National Registration number written in the spaces provided on page I in INK.

2. All the coupons in this book do not become valid at once. IT IS ILLEGAL TO USE ANY COUPON UNTIL IT HAS BEEN DECLARED VALID.

3. When shopping, you must not cut out the coupons yourself, but must hand this book to the shopkeeper and let him cut them out. IT IS ILLEGAL FOR THE SHOPKEEPER TO ACCEPT LOOSE COUPONS.

4. When ordering goods by post, do not send this book—cut the coupons out, and send them with your order BY REGISTERED POST.

5. If you join one of the Services take this book with you; it will be asked for. The Clothing Books of deceased persons must be handed to the Registrar of Births and Deaths when the death is notified.

6. This book is the property of H.M. Government and may only be used by or on behalf of the person for whom it is issued. TAKE GREAT CARE NOT TO LOSE IT.

PAGE II

TOKEN TOKEN

MAGENTA COUPONS

PAGE V

**Left:** This was a typical kit for a soldier of the Princess of Wales's Own Yorkshire Regiment in the First World War. It was packed into a small haversack and he marched off to war in the summer of 1914, confidently believing he would return by Christmas. Perhaps the most important piece of equipment he needed with him was not the obvious rifle. Boots became the real saviour for those consigned to spend months in the trenches. Even so, new ones would take time to break in and, since the soldiers had to march nearly everywhere, this would be very painful for their feet and might make a soldier unfit for service. The first battalions went to France equipped with shoes and gaiters, but they found that they lost their shoes in the cloying mud that sucked them from their feet. Many soldiers succumbed to trench foot, an infection caused by cold, wet and insanitary conditions. Men stood for hours on end in waterlogged trenches without being able to remove wet socks or boots. The feet would gradually go numb and the skin would turn red or blue. If untreated, trench foot could turn gangrenous and result in amputation. The only remedy for trench foot was for the soldiers to dry their feet and change their socks several times a day. By the end of 1915 British soldiers in the trenches had to have three pairs of socks with them and were under orders to change their socks at least twice a day.

**Below:** Hartlepool was hit by a double or even triple whammy during the First World War. Every town sent men off to the front, but there were not many that were also attacked by Zeppelins or shelled by enemy shipping. This group of soldiers from the Durham Light Infantry displayed some of the unexploded shells that were fired at the town in the episode that became known as 'the bombardment'. On 15th December 1914, a flotilla of warships sailed across the North Sea, or German Ocean as they would have it, intent on attacking the fortified towns on our east coast. Three cruisers peeled off from the main pack and opened fire on our unsuspecting town at just after 8 o'clock the following morning, as many local inhabitants were on their way to work. The guns were initially trained on the shore batteries and the lighthouse and the first shells cut all the lines of communications between the batteries throwing them into confusion. At first, locals thought that the noise of gunfire was our own ships indulging in some practice. It took some time before the townspeople realised what was happening, but they became all too aware when the docks were bombarded and armour piercing ordnance fell upon the houses behind them. Some 127 lost their lives, with over 400 suffering injuries.

**Above:** The Local Defence Volunteer (LDV) force was created in February 1940 by Walter Kirke, Commander in Chief of the Territorial Army. Winston Churchill had already asked the question of what would happen if 20,000 Wehrmacht troops were to land on the east coast and Kirke was aware that civilians could be on the front lines if the lessons of the invasion of Poland were to be learned. Formed initially to protect the coast around Dover, the LDV was launched as a national army in May when the War Secretary, Anthony Eden, broadcast to the nation, asking for more volunteers. The government was overwhelmed by the response as 250,000 men, largely drawn from the ranks of those too young or old to join up or those in reserved occupations, came forward. At first, there were some farcical sights as men drilled with broomsticks instead of rifles and confused the drivers of troop carriers by removing signposts. Patrols were undertaken using bicycles or on horseback. This period was the basis for the material used by Croft and Perry to write the BBC TV sitcom, 'Dad's Army'. The prime minister suggested a name change to Home Guard in late July and the force's role gradually shifted from an observational one to being more aggressive in its intent. Better equipment and sterner training lifted morale and the members' standing in the community. There is no doubt that they would have fought to the bitter end had it been necessary.

When the German Condor squadrons lent their assistance to Franco in the Spanish Civil War and brought a whole new perspective to the aerial aspect of warfare, the world took note. This was especially true after the destruction of Guernica, the picturesque Basque town that was virtually wiped off the map. Even though Prime Minister Chamberlain waved the little bit of paper he brought back from Munich, promising 'peace in our time', the realists knew that another war in Europe was imminent. They also appreciated that hostilities would include the bombing of industrial centres and cities and could possibly involve the use of gas and other noxious chemicals. Civil defence groups began organising their strategies and trained members in the use of measures that would help combat the effects of modern warfare on the civilian population. Centres were set up, like the one at Sherburn, where gas masks were assembled a whole year before war was officially declared. All schoolchildren were issued with them in the early summer of 1939 and they carried them in purpose-built boxes to and from lessons. Babies also had special helmets into which mothers would have to pump air with a bellows. On 31st August 1939, just four days before the formal declaration of war was made, Operation Pied Piper was put into action. Over the next few days, some 3,000,000 people were evacuated from the towns and cities marked down by the government as being at threat from enemy action. Most were children and long lines of them formed orderly queues at bus and railway stations. Carrying small, battered suitcases, along with ubiquitous gas masks, they had identification tags around their necks and made a heart rending sight as they left their parents and made their way to strange destinations in villages and more rural settings. The trauma of separation for these young evacuees, most of whom did not fully understand what was going on, stayed with many of them for years. Some had pleasant experiences, being welcomed into new homes with open arms. Others, though, were regarded as pests and intruders and made to feel unwanted. Some billets were quite out of the ordinary. A group of children from West Hartlepool's Lister Street School found a home at Mulgrave Castle, near Whitby. This is a mid 19th century building and the third to bear the name since the original 13th century castle was built. The evacuees were given a wing to themselves and even had servants looking after them. However, even though many of them experienced the luxury of hot running water for the first time, they felt lonely and missed their mums ever so much. Bed-wetting was a frequent sign of their insecurity. The Marchioness of Normanby, resplendent in her fur coat, greeted her guests with a smile, but she was not surprised to see most of the children return home before many months had passed.

The fashions of the early 1940s are evident in this picture. Not that fashion was uppermost in people's minds at this time. Something had caused the group - mainly of men and children - to gather on Bell Street. There is more than a whiff of curiosity at the presence of a photographer, particularly but not exclusively among the children in the foreground. It is possible that the crowds were out in 1940 as a result of the Hartlepools experiencing their first air raid of the Second World War. That sad event took place on 19th June 1940 and two people lost their lives. This was one of the first bombing raids on Britain during the conflict. Churchill had been appointed Prime Minister just a month before, and the outlook for the nation was dark and uncertain.

RDRESSER.
ACCONIST.
FECTIONER
SAGENT.
TOM NEWTON
SHAVING

**Above and right:** Only the elderly in our society can truly recall the sickening feeling of returning to a house that they had left earlier, only now to find it razed to the ground as they emerged from Anderson shelters or town centre basements. On 19th June 1940, the day dawned like any other. It was just 24 hours after Churchill had made his 'This was their finest hour' speech as the Battle of Britain was about to be fought in the skies over the south coast. Just after 11 pm, the sirens sounded and people scurried to get to some form of relative safety. There were a number who were foolhardy enough to think that this was another false alarm and they stayed put. They did not make that same mistake again. Some of them could not as they were among the 70 fatalities recorded during the 43 raids on the Hartlepools between June 1940 and March 1943. These photographs were taken on Friday, 21st June 1940 and, even this far removed from the time, we can understand something of the shock felt by the residents and workmen seen standing at the scene, surrounded by rubble and the smell of explosives and burning still tingling the nasal passages. But the weekend's work had only just begun. No sooner had the area been made safe and the worst of the damage cleared when back came the Luftwaffe. Enemy aircraft crossed the east coast at several places during the night. Bombs were dropped sporadically, though they seemed to be targeting those ports with particularly influential shipyards. The sound of the air raid siren, of enemy planes droning overhead and the whine of the bombs falling to ground became familiar during the long time ahead. We did not know it at the time, when the Hartlepools first came under attack, but this was the beginning of the period of the war that would come to be remembered as 'the Blitz'. At its height London and the Home Counties were under fire on 57 consecutive nights. The major portion of the Blitz occurred between September 1940 and May 1941, but no-one slept easy until peace was officially declared in 1945. By then, the number of civilian deaths was approaching six figures. This was part of Hitler's plan. He not only intended that his planes would destroy business and commercial targets essential to the economic survival of the country, but also that the ordinary man in the street would be demoralised, leading to a situation that would cause Britain to surrender. Thankfully, his was a plan that was never to succeed.

**Bottom:** The Women's Voluntary Service was founded as a Civil Defence auxiliary unit in 1938. The WVS gained much experience in providing emergency meals during the Second World War, often using the most primitive equipment. WVS mobile canteens served the forces both at home and abroad. During the war years the WVS gained an unenviable reputation amongst both members of the armed forces and those whose homes had been bombed, always ensuring that cups of tea, sandwiches and cakes were provided exactly where they were needed. When the war ended, however, members of the WVS had acquired a taste for public service and were unwilling simply to close shop. Distributing Meals on Wheels on a regular basis to needy people, particularly the elderly, after the war was a new challenge, but one the organisation readily adapted to. In the first six months of 1958, the year when this photograph was taken, the WVS delivered 75,000 such meals - the first course always piping hot from 'Hot Lock' containers. In this picture the WVS are looking delighted at the acquisition of two brand new vans. The fully-fitted vehicles named Cowan and Hanover are gaining the seal of approval from two key figures in WVS. Things had moved a long way from the immediate post-war years when members often delivered meals in their own vehicles.

**Left:** War had been declared, and every citizen of Britain, young and old, male and female, was called upon to put his or her back into the war effort. Those who did not go into military service of one kind or another worked in factories, dug for victory, gave up their aluminium baths and saucepans, joined organisations and aided in any way they could. These boys were not going to be left out; they might be too young to fight but while there were sandbags to be filled they were going to do their bit to protect their school building. Thousands of sandbags were used during World War II to protect the country and its beautiful civic buildings.

**Below:** Three people perished in the explosion on Church Street during one of the air raids that came during the summer blitz of 1940. Edgar Phillips' business, situated between the Clarence Hotel and the Yorkshire Penny Bank, was completely flattened. The attack on the night of 26th/27th August was one of many that month. It was just after midnight when Church Street was hit during assaults that ranged across County Durham and Northumberland. Sirens sounded in an almost daily procession and continued to do so for several months, though many of them were false alarms. Even so, the inhabitants were not to know this and nerves were stretched every time the wailing sound was heard. During this period some 43 raids on the twin Hartlepools were made. Although the aim was to destroy any industry which would help the British war effort, the bombs did not differentiate between shipyards or factories and houses, shops, churches and hotels. Older residents could claim that they lived through two bombardments, unlike many others in country. Most had only experienced attacks in World War Two, but over a quarter of a century earlier there had been shells flying across the Hartlepools as German ships opened fire. In a 40 minute bombardment in mid December 1914, the heavy cruisers 'Blucher', 'Seydlitz' and 'Moltke' fired over 1,000 shells into the towns.

**Above:** 'The day that the war broke out, the missus said to me ...', as Robb Wilton used to put it, it was time to think about self protection. Civil defence groups organised air raid drills and urged everyone to have a contingency plan for the occasions when enemy aircraft might come to call. Some had the foresight to have Anderson shelters installed in their back gardens, should they have such space at the rear of their properties. Named for the then Lord Privy Seal, John Anderson, they were designed in 1938 by Paterson and Kerrison. Designed to accommodate up to six people, they were constructed of both curved and straight galvanised, corrugated steel panels. Some had drainage sumps in the floor that allowed rainwater to drain away. They were buried in the soil for further protection and the earth that was banked up along the sides was often used to grow vegetables as residents did their bit in the Dig for Victory campaign. Householders fitted them out internally to their own particular requirements. Those earning less than £250 per annum received one free, while the more well off had to pay £7 out of their own pockets. Several hundred thousand were distributed before the war, with another 2 million being erected after hostilities commenced. Later, many were kept as children's dens or turned into garden sheds.

We're off, we're off, we're off in a motor car. Well, it was actually several charabancs, but let us not be picky. The Causeway Inn provided the backdrop for the large group of Stranton men off on a jolly in about 1925. Whether this was a works or pub outing is not clear, but we can be sure that they all had a good day out. Dressed in their best suits and either caps or hats as befitted their social status, there would be some ale supped and stories told if we are any judge of character. A ride on a motor coach, still a fairly recent phenomenon,

# EVENTS & OCCASIONS

became a rival to the day trip on the railway as it could provide door to door service. There was also the novelty effect and it was also another case of men and their toys, as we can still see in those opting for nights out in a stretch limousine today. But 80 or more years ago this was the equivalent. The men might have been headed for neighbouring Redcar or have loftier ambitions and be making for Whitby or the more distant Scarborough. Wherever they were bound, there would be tales to be told when they returned and things to be discussed over a pint or two at the Causeway on Saturday night.

**Above:** Cameron Memorial Hospital was a gift to West Hartlepool from the family of the brewer, John William Cameron (1841-97). He came to the town from Barnard Castle in 1865 to manage the Lion Brewery and took over its lease. As business boomed, a new brewery was required and this was built in 1892. Cameron also moved into local politics and in 1889 became West Hartlepool's third mayor. The hospital opened on Wooler Road/Serpentine Road in 1905 at a cost of over £20,000. With its well-equipped operating theatre, it was a state of the art facility at the time, many other hospitals being converted workhouses. Although a general hospital, it was relatively small having just 40 beds in the two wards. Children shared with adults as a 20 bed ward for them was not added until 1931. It became a training hospital two years later and was redesignated as a maternity hospital in 1955. It closed in 1991, was demolished and housing was built on the site. This Christmas scene from 1922 was taken on South Ward. Oh how the kiddies here would have longed to have been at home for the special day. But the doctors and nurses did their best to make the day special and Rudolph made a detour to bring Father Christmas to the ward just after lunch. For one lad the Memorial Hospital was his home for six long months following a serious accident. The 13-year-old Harry Waller is to the right of the ward sister and his family was to have a further connection with the Cameron as Harry's grandson was born on this very ward.

**Left:** Young children love to dance and it seems a shame that too few schools nowadays encourage the form of country dancing that many of us recall from our own early education. We listened to a school's broadcast on the radio that 'Miss' had taped and doh-si-doed and performed star turns to our hearts' content in the hall during the period our teacher called 'music, movement and mime'. At one time we had open air displays, like this one on the front at the Heugh, where youngsters showed off their skills for all to see. There were no self-conscious kiddies here as they were well used to enjoying themselves in such a lighthearted manner. They were able to use the steps and dances they learned when they went along with mum and dad to a church social or a barn dance. At such functions young Irene got used to the idea that a jolly dance with Uncle Bert breathing tobacco smoke all over her was part of a learning curve, just as little Eric learned to put up with Aunt Doris going on about him breaking a few hearts when he was older. However, the sight of two large ladies dancing the waltz together 'bust to bust', as Joyce Grenfell put it, was something for young minds to puzzle over.

**Above:** Seen on Lynn Street in about 1920, this highly decorated car was reminding passers-by of the forthcoming concert that was taking place the next night. Live variety, even of the amateur sort, was a very popular form of entertainment. The cinema was still in its infancy. Silent movies attracted sizeable audiences, but it was with the advent of sound at the end of the decade that the cinema started to rival and eventually overtake variety halls in popularity. Concerts, such as this one being advertised, tended to be held in any size of hall, from theatre down to a humble village hall. You could expect quite a varied level of talent as well as a variety of acts, including some rather quaint speciality acts. As well as the obvious singers, tap dancers and comics, there was every chance that there would be an animal act with a couple of dogs dressed in frilly collars jumping through hoops, pirouetting on their hind legs or riding a bike. At the lower end of the variety scale, there would be someone doing card tricks or rather obviously turning an umbrella into a bouquet of flowers. You could always spot the button he pushed to carry out that trick and naughty little boys in the audience were quick to tell him that they had spotted the ruse.

**Above:** The Co-op on the Headland was a fine example of the way the movement had developed since its conception as an idea in 1844 by the Rochdale Pioneers, who helped turned their little shop into an international concept. Hartlepool's version was a mammoth exercise by comparison as shoppers could purchase not just food, but furniture, linen, electrical items and all manner of hardware and ironmongery. Housewives collected the 'divvi' earned from shopping at the Co-op when they cashed in their completed cards, a useful addition to the family coffers in more difficult times. This developed from original rules that included distributing a share of profits according to purchases, making shoppers members rather than just customers. The Co-operative Wholesale Society (CWS) evolved from the North of England Co-operative Wholesale Industrial and Provident Society Limited. This was probably a sensible renaming as some of the profits would have gone to signwriters if that mouthful of a title had been retained. Having also set up its insurance and banking sections, the CWS entered the manufacturing world in 1873. It extended its influence overseas by buying up tea plantations in the Far East. By the turn of the century there were some 1,439 co-operative societies registered and the movement had come a long way since those Pioneers met up in East Lancashire.

**Below:** The bandstand at Hartlepool Headland was packed with local residents turning out to celebrate Empire Day in 1908. Although the world map was coloured red in large chunks of its surface and the empire was a source of immense pride to we Britons, the naming of 24th May as a special day of celebration was only instituted in 1902. The date was chosen to coincide with the birthday of Queen Victoria, who passed away the previous year, although suggestions about Empire Day had been first voiced during her Diamond Jubilee year in 1897. The event was intended to remind children that they 'might think with others in lands across the sea, what it meant to be sons and daughters of such a glorious Empire'. Even after its institution it was not universally observed as an annual event until 1916 at the height of the Great War. However, many countries had taken it on board and rejoiced in being part of one large family in a mood of togetherness that would last until the middle of the century. In the late 1940s and 1950s, as some of our former colonies severed the ties with independence or republicanism, the special day became pushed to one side. Empire Day was renamed British Commonwealth Day in 1958, with the first word being dropped all together in 1966. The date was twice changed before settling on the second Monday in March.

# Corus Tubes: A Shining Past, A Glittering Future

Corus Tubes is the largest manufacturer of steel tubes in North West Europe. Its products are used extensively in a very wide range of applications, from relatively small sizes used in diverse areas such as cars, furniture, central heating, sports equipment and sprinkler systems through to large sizes used in applications such as construction, earth moving equipment and the extraction and transport of oil and gas.

Corus Tubes has UK manufacturing sites in both Corby (business HQ) and Hartlepool. In addition, Corus Tubes also has manufacturing sites across Europe.

The use of pipe diameter sizes, expressed in inches, to name several of the UK Pipe Mills provides a simple means of identification, as well as indicating the maximum size of pipe that the Mills are designed to produce.

Though the name Corus is relatively new its local story goes back to the 19th century.

***Above:*** *West Hartlepool Steel & Iron Co. in 1890.* ***Below:*** *A bird's eye view of Cargo Fleet Works in the 1920s.*

Iron and steel making in the area began in Stockton around 1850. By 1890 the West Hartlepool Works was in full swing. In 1898 Sir William Gray, a Hartlepool shipbuilding magnate, and financier Christopher Furness, developed major steel manufacturing businesses which would, in 1900, become the South Durham Steel and Iron Company. In 1903 that company bought the Cargo Fleet Iron Company which, although having a lot of obsolete equipment, did have an excellent river frontage on the Tees.

In the 1920s a further purchase, insignificant at the time, but very significant in the light of later developments, was the Spun Iron Pipe Plant bought from Cochranes & Co based in north Ormesby.

The Spun Iron Plant literally spun molten iron centrifugally in a pipe mould until it gained the required shape and thickness, before being allowed to slowly cool. These pipes were traditionally accepted for the transportation of gas, oil, water and sewerage as they had the benefit of being resistant to corrosion, though to protect the pipes still further a coating was applied. This was the first venture into pipe making for the South Durham Iron and Steel Co.

Benjamin Talbot, a well-known metallurgist of the day, developed a new protective coating for the inside of pipes. The tar-like substance was applied in molten form.

The coating gave even greater protection from corrosion, but for technical reasons was found to be unsuitable for use in cast iron pipes.

In the early 1920s steel plate manufacturing was exceeding the needs of the market for ships and bridge building new markets were needed if the West Hartlepool Works were to be kept fully employed.

Happily the Talbot coating came to the rescue. Company engineer Isaac Williams and a Mr Mcquistan, a Director from Cochranes, began to manufacture and market pipes made from steel plate with Talbot coating.

As a result a new mill, known as the Stockton 84″ Pipe Mill, was built. The process was to roll cold steel plate in a 'mangle' until it formed a pipe shape; the joint was then welded shut.

The 84" Pipe Works was built in 1925. The pipes were welded using a water gas welding process. Water gas was made from coke, the flame from which was concentrated on the joint to weld the seam. The two edges were heated and pressed together. Once the pipe was welded it would be tested to ensure that it would not

***Top:*** *84″ Steel Pipe Works circa 1925.* ***Centre:*** *Talbot lined pipes.* ***Below:*** *Water gas welding.*

fail under pressure. Testing involved filling them with pressurised water and hitting them with a hammer – a method still in use today.

These were the first steel pipes to be produced by the South Durham Steel and Iron Co. The first pipes for commercial sale were sold to the Manchester Corporation for water. In 1927 the first export sale went to the Anglo-Persian Oil Company.

In Hartlepool the former Seaton Carew Iron Works, subsequently known as the North Works, was in its heyday.

With nowhere to expand at North Works a new site had to be found for the expansion of iron and steel making and plate rolling for the South Durham Steel and Iron Co.

The site chosen was the Greatham airport.

This new development began in the 1950s and was to become a fully integrated works. In the late 1960s, with the integrated works now in full swing, it was decided to build yet another pipe mill. This was to be the 44″ Pipe Mill.

The gas supply industry now needed many new pipelines, not only for the main gas supplies from the North Sea but also the new distribution lines within towns and cities. The latter were to be of much smaller diameter, and so the opportunity arose to create a new 20″ Pipe Mill that could supply pipes within a range of 8″ to 20″ diameter.

***Top left***: *Pipe hydrotesting with the use of a hammer.* ***Top right:*** *Hot pipe end socketting.* ***Below:*** *Cast iron pipes replaced with steel pipes.*

1991 and 1998 making it one of the most technically respected pipe mills in the world. In addition to pipelines the 20″ Mill also had the advantage of being able to produce a range of structural products in a square, rectangular and round form. These products, still produced today, are made by heating the round tube to a normalising temperature of 950 degrees Celsius and then hot-forming the pipe into the finished shape.

Major applications for these products include: Kansai Airport (Japan), various football stadia including Wembley, Arsenal's Emirates Stadium, Cardiff Millennium Stadium and the London Eye amongst others.

Meanwhile enormous commercial and political pressures were building up to rationalise and nationalise Britain's steel industry. The three key players in the North East were South Durham, Stewart and Lloyds, and Dorman Long. The Benson Committee set up by the British Iron and Steel Federation had recommended the creation of a single steel complex on Teesside.

The anticipated demand for pipes to exploit North Sea gas finds was so large that immediate measures to expand production were matters of national importance. On this ground alone the merger of the three companies was urgent. Proposals for the merger and the creation of British Steel and Tube Ltd were announced in November 1966.

The new 20″ Pipe Mill, commissioned in 1967, was built for Stewart and Lloyds.

Pipes made from steel coil up to 20″ in diameter were eminently suitable for the thousands of miles of gas pipeline being installed all across the country. The 20″ Pipe Mill has subsequently had multi-million pound upgrades in 1985,

***Top left:*** *Hartlepool North Works 14th June 1937.* ***Above:*** *The site steam locomotive in the late 1950s early 1960s, subsequently donated to Beamish Museum.* ***Below, left and right:*** *Interior and exterior welding.*

Hartlepool, and the 84″ mill at Stockton.

By the late 1980s a new Pipe Mill was required in the 42″ diameter range as the existing 44″ Pipe Mill was found to be too weak for new customer demand for deep offshore gas and oil pipelines. The new Pipe Mill was bought second-hand from Japan and became the Hartlepool 42″ Pipe Mill.

On the 3rd December 1987 the UK Government formally announced its intention to privatise the British Steel Corporation.

Corus was formed on 6th October 1999 through the merger of British Steel and Koninklijke Hoogovens, a Netherlands based company.

***Left:*** *Construction stages (small pictures) and the completed (large picture) South Works showing both 20″ & 44″ Pipe Mills.* ***Below:*** *Expanding operation.* ***Bottom:*** *From left to right: Internal view of 44″ Pipe Mill, coil supply to pipe forming and welding at 20″ Mill, 42″ Pipe Mill welding and hot rolling at 84″ Pipe Mill.*

In March 1974 the Minister of State for Industry, Lord Beswick, initiated a review of British Steel's corporate strategy. Particular emphasis was placed on the rationalisation programme (intended to save £170 million over two years) including the proposed closure of several steel plants.

The late 1970s through to the 1980s saw the final closure of operations at the North Works; the final plants to go were the blast furnaces, coke ovens and sinter plant in 1978. This was followed by the gradual closures of the South Works following the Lord Beswick Report and the Redcar Developments then taking place. The final plants to go at the South Works were the coke ovens and the plate mill.

All that remained of the old South Durham Steel and Iron Co were the three pipe mills: the 20″ and 44″ pipe mills at

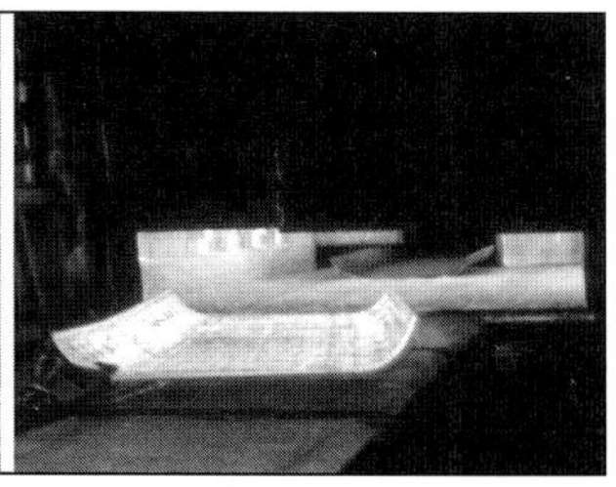

On 2nd April 2007 Corus became part of Tata Steel group, one of the most profitable steel companies in the world.

Today the Tata Group has more than 246,000 employees across 96 operating companies; it is one of the world's largest enterprises, covering steel, engineering, energy, materials, chemicals, consumer products (including Tetley Tea), communications, information systems and the automotive sector. In 2008 Tata was the leading bidder to buy both Jaguar and Landrover, as well as announcing its own highly acclaimed 4-seater 'Nano' car priced at only £1,300.

Despite the change of ownership, for now, the name Corus Tubes continues. The word Corus is Latin for something which shines. The firm has enjoyed a shining past and looks forward with confidence to an equally glittering future.

***Top left:*** *An oval support column from the Corus Celsius range.* ***Top centre and top right:*** *A select few of huge projects which have been built with pipes and tubing from Corus Tubes. Pictured are: The Millennium Stadium, Cardiff, (centre), and the London Eye.* ***Above left:*** *27 metre pipes ready for despatch by road to Wick.* ***Below:*** *Hartlepool Works, 2008.*

How can you not be nostalgic when viewing such magnificent old vehicles? There are few of us left who could manage to remember seeing them in their heyday, but that still does not prevent us from finding them both quaint and important at the same time. They are part of the history of the last century and evocative of the times in which the oldest in our society grew up. We must preserve such images as they are part of the lifestyle in which older generations or those of our parents and grandparents were moulded. Consequently, they affect those of us who are less long in the tooth as well. You have to realise that such wagons and trolley buses were very modern when seen on our roads in the mid 1920s. It must have been a bit of a boneshaking ride as suspension systems were not what they are today. The narrow tyres and generally slim, box like design of the vehicles might bring a smile to our lips as we compare them with what we can see on the road in the 21st century, but at least they were on the move. We might have come a long way when it comes to refining and improving performance, but what good is that when you are stuck in a traffic jam on the A19? The Railless trolley bus on the left was accompanied by the tower wagon that was used to erect and service the overhead wires.

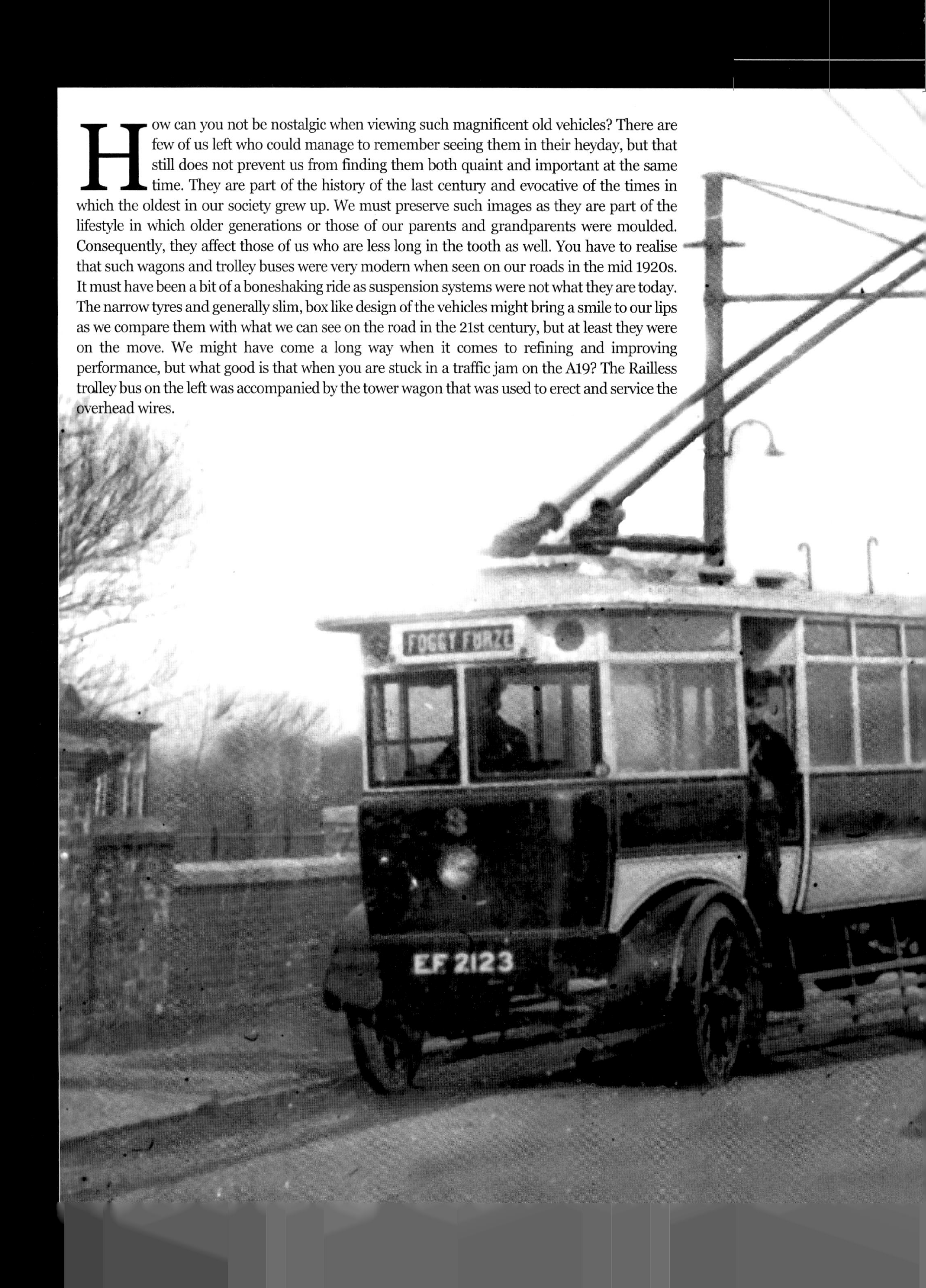

# TRANSPORT

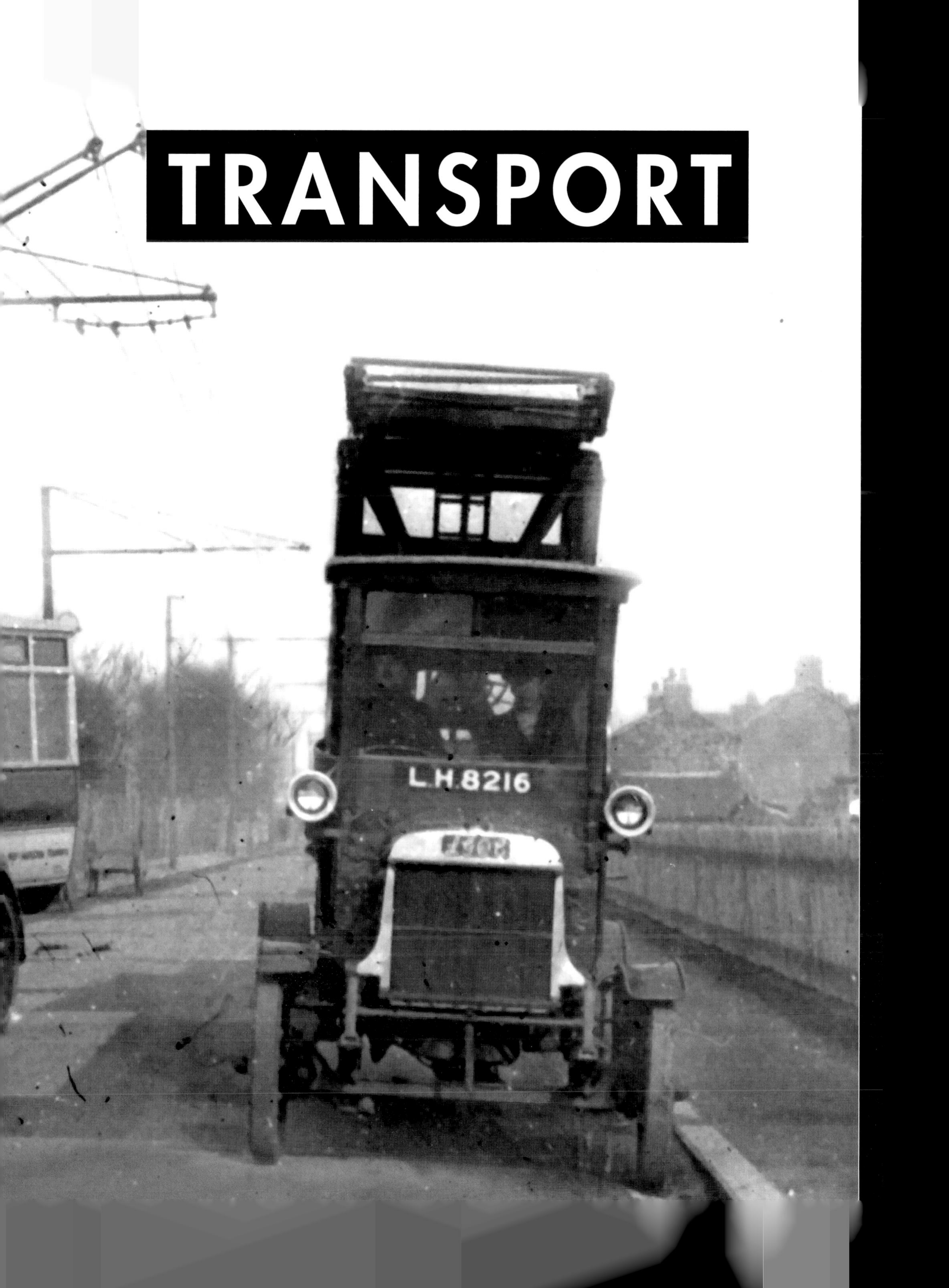

**Above:** This tram was decked out to look like one of the German submarines that were part of the modern face of warfare in the 1914-18 conflict. Times had changed since the great European powers had last taken to the battlefield in any meaningful way. Cavalry charges and lines of infantry deciding skirmishes and battles in a matter of a few days were for the history books. By the time the Armistice was signed, air power, tanks and submarines would more than have made their mark as the horses were put out to graze and soldiers floundered in their trenches. The first submersible was demonstrated on the Thames in the early 17th century by Cornelius Drebbel, but it is thought to have been little more than a bell being towed by a boat, though improved versions were tested in the 1650s. Development was slow as they relied upon human power to propel them, but several were used successfully 200 years later during the American Civil War. Mechanically powered submarines were in use in the late 19th century, but it was with the move to diesel electric engines as the next century began that these craft came into their own. During the Great War, most submarines operated for long stretches on the surface of the water, but they were an effective war tool and responsible for the infamous sinking of the Lusitania in 1915 that helped bring the USA into the war.

**Below:** Stop me and buy one. Perhaps not, but this police motor tricycle, seen at Wingate in about 1920, must have turned a few heads when it was driven along the road. At least you saw a bobby on the beat, even if this one looked more like part of a music hall act. Motor tricycles were quite common during this early part of our 20th century transport history. The NSU machine originated in Germany, manufactured by the Neckarsulm Strickmaschinen Union. Not surprisingly, the vehicle was sold using the company's initials. It would have taken a tricycle of charabanc proportions to carry the full title otherwise. Originally a knitting machine business, the German firm began making motor cycles in 1901. In World War II it brought out one of the weirdest pieces of military ordnance ever seen. This was a light armoured vehicle with the front end of a motorcycle attached to the rear end of a half-track. Conventional NSU motorbikes competed in the Isle of Man TT races after the war. Returning to our policeman and his machine, this knowledgeable custodian of the law would have been aware that the very first motor cycles did have three wheels. Edward Butler, an English inventor, produced one in 1884, though it was Gottlieb Daimler's designs that popularised motor cycles from 1895 onwards. In Britain, BSA, Ariel and Norton all manufactured tricycles in their early days until the two wheeled versions dominated the market.

**Left:** Was HG Wells inspired to create his Martian machines along these lines when he wrote 'War of the Worlds' and did John Christopher (Samuel Youd) get his idea for the Tripods in the series of books that began with 'The White Mountains' from this photograph? Obviously not, but we can be forgiven flights of such fancy when looking at a long rank of trolley buses. After all, to modern eyes, they do look rather incongruous with their trailing arms and pantographs. We can imagine them as creatures from outer space, sucking the life blood, or in their case the electricity, out of the cables that criss-crossed the streets in the middle years of the last century. Hartlepool purchased the tramway within its boundary and began operating trolleybuses under the Corporation Trolley Vehicles Act of 1926. The first ones were Railless four wheelers with 36-seater bodywork built by Short Brothers. In April 1938, a major investment in new high capacity double-deckers was undertaken. These Daimler CTM models, with Roe 54-seater bodies, were photographed at Greenland on 23 April 1939. Much to the annoyance of Hartlepool Corporation, West Hartlepool decided to phase out its trolleys in the late 1940s, gradually replacing them with new motorbuses. On 3rd April 1953, the last of this icon of the second quarter of the 20th century's style of public transport made its final journey.

**Below centre:** Pictured at the start of the 1920s, this Bristol single-decker was part of the local transport fleet that boasted the very best in modern passenger travel. In this decade the bus superseded the trolley and the tram in importance as it was more flexible and served the expanding needs of the local people far better. Trams were phased out and double-decker buses were then introduced in the early 1930s when a fleet of Daimlers took to the road. Trolley buses disappeared in the 1950s, leaving the motor bus to reign supreme. The Bristol in the photograph was on Cliff Terrace, on the Headland. Behind it are the 19th century townhouses that have had a wonderful sea view for well over 100 years. The two Hartlepool boroughs operated their transport services jointly during the tram years, but Hartlepool went its own way when the trams stopped running, operating a fleet of buses with a blue livery, banded in cream. However, with local government reorganisation looming, the two fleets were reunited in April 1967. Maroon and cream then dominated the scene.

**Right:** This canteen bus dates from World War II and would have given excellent service during those years. Soldiers waiting in long lines ready to embark on service across the Channel or to the more distant shores of North Africa waited patiently for their turn. Their stomachs were filled with food brought to them by mobile canteens that drove up and down filling the inner man. Often driven by women, the converted buses clocked up many a mile. They were also used in our towns following an enemy raid during the blitz

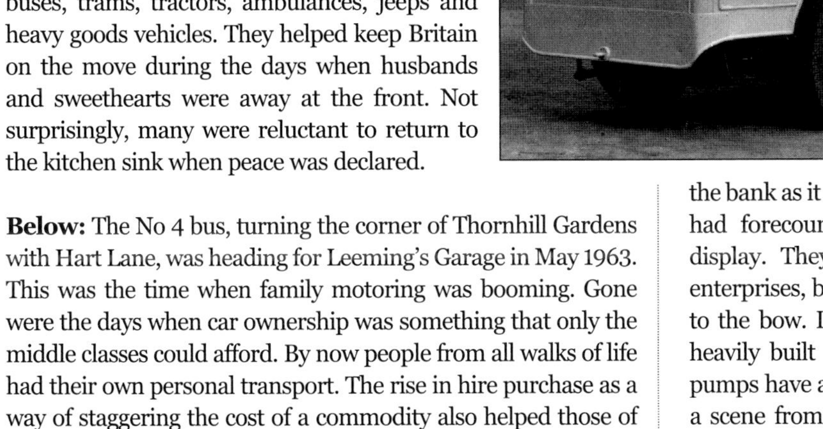

years. People rendered homeless, firemen, the police and ambulance crews gave thanks for warm food and a hot beverage that was dispensed from these canteens by willing volunteers, such as members of the Women's Voluntary Service. The so-called weaker sex contributed to the war effort as part of the voluntary and formal civil defence units that the prime minister later referred to as 'the army that Hitler forgot'. Female drivers took over from their male counterparts behind the wheels of buses, trams, tractors, ambulances, jeeps and heavy goods vehicles. They helped keep Britain on the move during the days when husbands and sweethearts were away at the front. Not surprisingly, many were reluctant to return to the kitchen sink when peace was declared.

**Below:** The No 4 bus, turning the corner of Thornhill Gardens with Hart Lane, was heading for Leeming's Garage in May 1963. This was the time when family motoring was booming. Gone were the days when car ownership was something that only the middle classes could afford. By now people from all walks of life had their own personal transport. The rise in hire purchase as a way of staggering the cost of a commodity also helped those of seemingly humble backgrounds to get behind the wheel. In real terms, family saloons were much cheaper than they had been in earlier decades and the cost of petrol did not threaten to break the bank as it has in the 21st century. Garages such as Leeming's had forecourts where easily affordable runabouts were on display. They still had their workshops and filling station enterprises, but car dealership was developed as an extra string to the bow. Looking at the scene, which today is much more heavily built up as new estates have been erected, the petrol pumps have a lovely, dated appearance. They seem to belong to a scene from Toytown or Trumpton and only need Noddy to drive up in his yellow car with its red wings to complete the picture. An attendant can just be seen filling up a car with Regular, or whatever the choice might have been.

**Above:** The electric trolley bus first appeared on Hartlepool's streets in 1923. It could use the cabling that belonged to the trams but, of course, did not require the metal tracks at ground level. This made it a more versatile vehicle and one that needed less maintenance. Not every pedestrian was in favour as some had close shaves with the trolley that seemed to creep up on them unawares as they ambled across the street. The old trams made a clanking noise that warned of their approach, but the trolley just glided along the road like some form of whispering death for those who did not have eyes in the backs of their heads. This example of West Hartlepool's transport system of about 1927 was heading for one of the most unusually named places in Britain, never mind just our town. Foggy Furze suggests that it was called after a mist-shrouded gorse bush, but the derivation of the name is possibly a little more complex. In Victorian times it had been referred to as Foggy Furrows. Fogg is an old Norse word for grass and there actually is a grass variety known as Yorkshire Fog. Perhaps then, rather than a place where gorse bushes grew, Foggy Furze may have evolved from a name for ploughed fields where rough grass grew.

**Below:** The Daimler-Bedford bus, bodywork by Roe, stood at the Stockton Road and Ashgrove Avenue junction, towards the south of West Hartlepool, ready to depart for Wynyard Road. Those of us who are in middle age and grumble about the behaviour of young people today should take a hard look at the picture. Taken in the early 1960s, this is just what we were doing 45 or so years ago. Did we queue politely as we expect kids to do nowadays? That is a rhetorical question as the answer is plain to see. Pity the poor woman attempting to board in the midst of the scrum that had formed around her. The conductor seems to have alighted from the bus in order to try to instil some form of crowd control into the unruly mob. His lack of success is apparent. So, the next time someone tells you that the youth of today lack discipline and have no respect for authority, put this image under his nose. If memory serves us well, we can remember that the only time we lined

up properly at the bus stop was when the head came out to supervise the proceedings. Known quite simply as 'the boss', just a stern look from him was all that was required to cow even the wildest rebel. Thinking back to our schooldays, those short trousers bring back memories of chapped legs in the winter and scabby knees all the year round.

**Below:** The array of buses near Haverton shipyard was waiting for a shift to finish in 1959. When the hooter blew workers streamed in their hundreds towards the fleet of vehicles waiting to whisk them off home for their evening meal and a well earned pint or two at the working men's club later on. The deafening din of hammers upon steel drowned out most other sounds in the industrial heyday of the north-east shipbuilding and repair yards. Such companies as Swan Hunter employed thousands of workers who toiled to produce over 1,600 ships for this particular employer which first went into business at Wallsend in the 1880s. The Haverton yard closed in about 1980, but was back in the news 25 years later when the site was earmarked for redevelopment as an order to build a £300 million drilling rig and platform was placed. Hartlepool's own shipbuilding interest began with the Hartlepool General Shipping Company's 'Castle Eden' in 1836. It ended in 1961 when the 'Blanchland', built by William Gray, was launched. The intervening years saw the change from wooden sailing vessels to the iron steamships and steam tankers that would provide the backbone of the town's prosperity for over a century. All this took place around a harbour that was once so silted up that grain was harvested here in the late 18th century.

**Below:** The single-decker Corporation bus was packed with passengers heading off into town. In the years that followed the Second World War, people found life difficult. Although there was euphoria in mid-1945 when the hostilities ceased, the celebratory mood did not last long. The country was almost bankrupt and in hock to the Americans to such a degree that the war debt would not be completely wiped off the slate for another 60 years. Rationing restrictions were tighter than ever and wage packets remained slim as companies, both private and public, tried to rebuild their businesses, both in terms of their order books and the actual bricks and mortar. There was little spare cash lying around for the ordinary man in the street to spend on such fripperies as motor cars. He and his missus went on the bus, whether it was to work, the shops or for an evening at the pictures. His children were not ferried to and from school in mammoth people carriers. They also hopped on board, or simply walked the required distance to their classrooms and thought little of it. Buses were always crowded and standing room only was often the case if you got on halfway along the route. At least, though, there was always some gentleman or child happy to offer a seat to a woman or pensioner.

**Above:** Row, row, row your boat, gently down the stream. In this instance it was a case of across the bay from one Hartlepool to another. This was the view as the ferry approached old Hartlepool from the Middleton side and dates from about 1910. This sort of service existed for hundreds of years and a written record of 1600 describes one William Porrett being paid to provide a 'fferiboote' across the waters. Some readers will still recall travelling on it as this one continued until 1953. Passengers were trusted to drop their pennies for the fare onto a plate located near the stern. As the crow flies, or boat rowed, it is only 100 yards from the Headland to the mainland, but a much lengthier journey by road. For years shipyard workers used the ferry to get to and from the docks rather than walk a mile or so around the marshy area known as the Slake. The crossing was not without its risks. When the shipyards were an important feature of Hartlepool life the bay was busy with naval traffic. Taking a small boat into such an environment required skilful navigation, even over such a short distance, and there were a small number of accidents, including fatalities, that occurred. As the docks and engine works went into decline the ferry became as redundant as the workers it served.

# BIRDS EYE VIEW

**Centre:** A 1946 aerial view looking down Church Street from the top of Christ Church tower. Everything is peaceful, quiet and normal. It is hard to imagine that only a short time ago things were very different. During the war there would have been hardly any cars as petrol was rationed. Windows would have tape criss-crossed over them to stop them shattering when the bombs dropped. Shops would have been almost empty as everything was in short supply (as would still have been the case at the time of this photograph as there was still rationing). People in the streets would all be carrying gas masks and listening for air raid sirens. At night there would not be a single light showing so as not to give the enemy aeroplane a target to attack.

**Top right:** This photograph dates from the late 1940s and shows a view of Hartlepool long before it was transformed by the construction of the Middleton Grange Shopping Centre. The foreground of the picture is dominated by All Saints Church at Stranton, just the shortest of walks away from the 1852 Lion Brewery which was built by William Waldon. Waldon died shortly after the brewery was completed and the business eventually passed into the hands of a trusted employee by the name of Cameron. The rest, as they say, is history. Stockton Street is the broad thoroughfare running across the bottom of the picture. Roughly opposite the brewery stood a popular cinema. Probably known by readers as the Gaumont it was originally

This was the first local cinema to show a 'talking' film, a very well supported event which took place in 1929. Keen eyes may just be able to make out the outline of the

**Bottom right:** The delights of the one way system are here for us to see. It is every highways planner's dream. Throw in a few modern mini roundabouts and speed bumps, with a sprinkling of road narrowing for added spice, and he is in heaven. If that is not enough, then what about a dedicated bus lane or two? It does not matter that locals and visitors alike have difficulty in coping with all these innovations just as long as the highways people feel that they have achieved something. Usually it is a mixture of chaos, traffic jams and busted shock absorbers. This is one of the earliest attempts to mess with motorists. Seen towards the end of the 1960s this part of the town in front of Christ Church had been designated as a one way route. It is rumoured that there is the ghost of a Ford Anglia still circling Upper Church Street that can be seen on dark and misty nights looking for an escape route. The buildings in this vicinity still look much as they were in years gone by, but of course the planners have been at it again in the meantime. Perhaps they were disappointed that traffic managed to work its way through here successfully and actually make it out onto Stockton Street. So, it was blocked off and pedestrianised. Try to drive you

**Left:** In 1970 the decade began with us in an era of flower power and turning towards peace rather than war. Even so, the Vietnam War was still raging and Arab terrorists were blowing up hijacked planes in the Jordanian desert. At home, the Tories returned to power when Ted Heath won a surprise victory, but it was all about to end in tears for the Beatles as they sought to wind up their collaboration in the law courts. On Church Street, life carried on quietly as before. Looking down towards the railway line and distant harbour area, the scene looked very peaceful. Parked cars at the kerbside remind us that there was a time when double yellow lines did not cover the edges of highways. Ralph Ward Jackson surveyed the sight from his tapered limestone plinth at the top of the street. The bronze statue, depicting him in a frock coat with one hand on his hip and the other held out to the side, looks east across the town that he helped to shape. Colonel Cameron, chairman of the Lion Brewery, presented the monument to the town in 1897, the year of Queen Victoria's Diamond Jubilee. It was unveiled by the Marquis of Londonderry in front of a crowd of over 2,000. The black covering on the statue was applied in the late 20th century as a protection against verdigris that was attacking the bronze.

**Below:** Despite all the modern technology of radar, satellite tracking and onboard computers, ships still need to have the backup of traditional lighthouses. They have helped save so many millions of tons of shipping and countless lives down the years by warning of the dangers around coastlines. The work of the lighthouse keeper has, at times, been inspirational and none more so than in the Grace Darling story. In 1838, this daughter of the keeper of Longstone Lighthouse on the Farne Islands helped rescue sailors from the stricken 'Forfarshire'. Lighthouses have been around for thousands of years. Perhaps the most well known is the one built at Alexandria in 280 BC. However, it was not until the 17th century that these maritime aids came to be an important part of the coastal way of life. In England, Trinity House built its first in 1613, with the famous Eddystone Lighthouse being constructed in 1698. Keepers had an arduous and responsible job in trimming wicks, replenishing fuel, winding clockworks and carrying out such necessary regular maintenance as cleaning lenses and windows. The first lighthouse on The Heugh was built by Stephen Robinson and was lit for the first time on 1st October 1847. It was taken down in 1915 to allow the nearby gun battery clear sight of the sea. The new one, seen here in 1930, was built in 1926 and powered by electricity that gave out a light the equivalent of over 60,000 candles.

**Above:** The photographer had come out onto the roof of Binns' department store in 1962 to take this view across West Hartlepool, looking along Upper Church Street to Christ Church and then beyond to the coast. The church was still operating as a religious centre at the time but had little more than a decade to serve the town before it closed as the congregation numbers fell. This was caused by a mixture of house clearance reducing the number of parishioners and a general falling-off in attendances experienced by churches across the country. Christ Church was the first church built to cater for the newly-arrived population of West Hartlepool, for which we can thank its founder Ralph Ward Jackson. After the opening of the first dock and harbour in 1847 the population multiplied dramatically. By 1851 there were over 4,000 people working in the new town; in the next ten years this would increase to over 29,000. Jackson believed that it was his responsibility to provide for the spiritual needs of the town. He took it upon himself to find the money to build the church. EB Lamb, a London architect, produced the first designs, but they were too large and expensive. By 1854, new plans were actioned and the church consecrated by the Bishop of Durham, with prayers being led by the new vicar, John Hart Burges.

**Below:** As we entered the so-called swinging-sixties, life was changing for most of us and, generally speaking, for the better. The austerity of the major part of the previous postwar years had been put behind us and we looked forward to the lifestyle that Prime Minister Macmillan referred to in his famous 'never had it so good' speech. As we enjoyed more money in our pay packets, the world seemed a brighter place. We dressed accordingly and out went the drab greys and dull blacks that our parents wore, to be replaced with pastel shades and bouncy hairdos instead of the tight perms that were once the fashion. Two-tone motor cars drove down the street, some with outrageous rear fins that mirrored the brash style of the Americans whom many copied. Despite the influence of our cousins across the big pond, we were also able to develop our own individuality. Whilst Elvis was still king, home-produced music became more popular. Even if Eric Burdon had to go to Louisiana for the theme of the million selling 'House of the rising sun', it was his Animals, from just up the coast on Tyneside, who topped the charts on both sides of the Atlantic in 1964. At that time the United depot and bus station was still a busy place, with beyond it the timber dock, where the HMS Warrior was later restored, and its neighbours bustling with trade.

Natural gas from the North Sea has been part of our lives for over four decades. The area from which we get this resource has become the centre of one of the world's most productive energy industries. Gas was first found in quantity in the Groningen area of the Netherlands in 1959. Britain's involvement in the industry was kick-started by the discovery of gas in the West Sole field, off the coast of East Anglia, by the BP jack-up drilling rig Sea Gem, late in 1965. The excitement was tempered by the capsizing of the rig just days later and the 13 fatalities were a stark reminder of the perils of working at sea. Until the sea bed was tapped we relied on traditional methods of production, as in the Northern Gas Making Plant seen here under construction in January 1964. The allied discovery of oil provided hope for the former shipyard workers in the Hartlepools who had fallen on hard times as jobs disappeared from in front of their faces. Unemployment was in double percentage figures and rising. Although the new gas and oil companies could not take everyone under their wings, out at sea or at the terminals on land, at least they would come to lend a helping hand as this decade and the next one unfolded.

# AT THE DOCKS

This sweeping panorama of the docks shows the once thriving maritime industry in full swing. The warehouses would have been bursting with goods waiting to be moved on inland or, alternatively, out across the ocean to far and distant lands. Large cargo ships were berthed, awaiting the loading and unloading of the merchandise that provided the source of much of the economy of the twin towns. Tug boats bustled backwards and forwards, helping the bigger vessels negotiate their way to the quayside. The various dock areas were linked by railway lines that snaked away towards the hinterland as the whole area throbbed with activity. Similar scenes could be captured all along the north-east coast as some of the country's main shipping industries were situated here. The trio of rivers, Tees, Wear and Tyne, all hosted yards that boasted their own particular brand of success. Many of the local inhabitants relied upon the docks for their employment, whether it be directly linked with the sea or indirectly via associated jobs. Sons followed fathers and grandfathers into the shipyards and, for several generations, it seemed that life would always be so. As a maritime nation it appeared that such a way of life would go on forever.

**Above:** Pictured in 1900, the Headland view across to the walls and the town beyond is one of peace and tranquillity. It may have seemed so as this moment was frozen in time, with the waters like a millpond and the fishing boats tied up for the day, but there was often a hustle and a bustle about the place as men brought home their catches and prepared them for sale at the quayside. As its name suggests, the Headland is a peninsula, surrounded by the sea on three sides. While its industrial links with the rest of the world has put West Hartlepool firmly within the influence of the River Tees, the old town maintained a form of both attitudinal and legislative independence for a long time until it was pushed into amalgamation in the 1960s. The area around the Headland relied on the sea and not the river. In prehistoric times this magnesium limestone land had probably been a forested tidal island and successive generations of inhabitants continued to regard themselves as being apart from the rest of the world. When West Hartlepool came into existence in the mid-1800s, those established in the old town viewed their new neighbours with some disdain as 'incomers'. Some say that the attitude still persists among older families.

**Below:** The fishing nets were hung out to dry on the sea wall and the cobles had been dragged or lifted ashore at Fish Sands in this evocative snapshot of a way and pace of life that has long disappeared. Taken just over a century ago in 1907, this photograph is part of the heritage of our old town. Never mind that the monkey was strung up near here for that is just an aside. What is far more important about this stretch of the coast is that it is intrinsically connected with the very essence of how people earned their living and worked together as a community. Over by the wall, fish that had been caught were being prepared for sale in a way that had existed for hundreds of years before. Since medieval times the catch was gutted and cleaned and got ready for the market or for fishwives to hawk around the streets. The modern quay at Fish Sands was built in 1880, but some of the fishermen still preferred to sit by the sea wall, close to where they had landed their boats, just as they and their fathers had done in earlier times. The little children playing at the water's edge also had a role to fulfil as they would soon learn the art of net mending and fish filleting.

Vessels both large and small have been important in the history of the Hartlepools. Grand sailing ships once called at the docks and the memory of their heritage is preserved in the museum area at the marina today. The HMS Trincomalee is a remarkable example of the era when Britain ruled the seas, both in terms of warfare and in trade. Built in Bombay, it was launched in 1817 and made the lengthy journey across the seas to Portsmouth. However, as the threat from the 'little corporal', Napoleon, had subsided, it lay in harbour in semi-retirement for a quarter of a century before undertaking service as a Royal Navy frigate in the Americas and, later, in the Crimea. In 1862 she was berthed at West Hartlepool as a training ship and moved to Southampton in 1877. After further service that lasted over a century, she returned here where restoration work was commenced to turn the grand old lady into the focus of the town's Maritime Experience. In the foreground of this photograph we can see some of the smaller boats that were once regular sights bobbing up and down on the waves of the North Sea. The ones we know as 'cobles' were part and parcel of a fisherman's existence along the east coast of northern England. They were privately owned and launched by family members from the beach rather than the harbour.

The aerial photograph of the Headland was taken in 1930 at a time when the country's economic depression was approaching its worst days. The social divide became even more marked as we saw poverty, with its images of lines of unemployed men, rows of shabby houses and undernourished children in back streets, juxtaposed with prosperity. The middle classes enjoyed electrical appliances, motorcars and dinner dances as they grew further apart form those who had toiled to provide their wealth. The depression was largely fuelled by the stock market crash in America in the late 1920s, but was exacerbated in Britain by a fall-off in

trade made worse by heavy import taxes and a failure to update working practices and plant in our industries. As trade dropped the need for transport fell. Ships and railway rolling stock were needed less and less. The towns and cities that relied on these industries were badly affected and government measures to control the situation only made matters worse. Income tax was raised for those in work and unemployment benefit cut for those out of work. The decline in the fortune of Hartlepool's shipyards had already been felt in the previous decade, but it would not get any better in the 1930s. Gray's, one of the town's main employers, built no ships at all in 1931 and 1933.

**Below:** The dockside could be a dirty, gloomy place, but the industrial revolution taught us that there is money in grime. It was not called 'filthy lucre' without good reason. This bleak view certainly suggests that work here was not one of aesthetics, but stark practicalities. This was a workplace where you did your shift and enjoyed the rest of the day away from this environment. The rail trucks act as a good reminder that ships and locomotives were intrinsically linked from the middle of the 19th century onwards. It was in our region that the first commercial rail operations were begun on any scale, though part of the inspiration goes back further than most people think. Even though the first steam railway service was not opened until 1825, the principles of early railway date back much earlier to Blyth in Northumberland. Wagonways can be dated as far back as 1609 when they were used to transport coal from the mines at Bedlington to the coast and the River Blyth. Although they proved unsuccessful the germ of the idea had been born. After Trevithick's work with steam locomotives in Coalbrookdale and South Wales in the early 1800s, it was Edward Pease who was the driving force behind the opening of the Stockton and Darlington Railway in 1825. The use of this new form of transportation opened up easy access to the ports from the coalfields and the likes of West Hartlepool and its docks came into their own.

**Above:** About 150 yards along the promenade from the Headland lighthouse are the feet of what was once a talking point for visitors here. That is all that now remains of Elephant Rock, photographed in the year before it collapsed in a raging storm on 10th May 1891. This natural curiosity enabled many a fanciful dad to spin a yarn or two about it to his children. Who knows? Perhaps Rudyard Kipling was inspired to write one of his Just So stories after hearing about Hartlepool's Headland feature. It is possible that many local residents might not have seen a real elephant for themselves until after this one was washed away. We seem to have a fascination for strange animal shapes. We look into the sky and see clouds that take on the appearance of whichever animal we fancy as no one else can ever see what it is we think we have spotted. Then there are the various horses etched into our hills in several locations across the countryside, not to mention the figure locally known as the 'rude man' at Cerne Abbas in Dorset. Goodness knows what the Victorians made of that last particular carving.

**Above:** As the crow flies, or perhaps the fish swims, it is only about 100 yards across the water from the Headland to the mainland. The ferry saved residents a cross-country walk of well over a mile as the alternative route meant taking a detour on foot around the marshland of the Slake. Being rowed across the water saved both time and shoe leather. Although the ferry was well used by shipyard workers coming from the Headland to the West Hartlepool docks, it had been in use for hundreds of years before Ward Jackson started to create the new town. It provided easy access to the coast road along the sands towards Stockton. Travelling in this manner across the water was not without its problems as the north-east weather could always be relied upon to throw up more than its fair share of rainstorms that made the crossing a necessary but damp experience. The Corporation ran ferryboats and hired retired fishermen to crew them. Passenger numbers dwindled as parts of the Slake were turned into docks and workers could walk along new pathways. In 1939 the Corporation withdrew from running a service and turned it over to its employees, who continued in business until 1952, when running costs and the developments in private and public transport made the ferry an uneconomic venture. The photograph dates from 1910.

**Right:** The shipyard at Graythorpe was never a pretty spot, with its berths for loading scrap metal and the paraphernalia and detritus of the shipbuilding industry. In more recent times the area has been the object of much heated discussion about the dismantling of American 'ghost ships' that contained toxic waste and were regarded by many as floating timebombs. This aerial photograph of the river estuary, looking north towards Seaton Carew, was taken in 1974, long after its heyday as a maritime yard. William Cresswell Gray, son of the founder of the Central Marine Engine Works, extended the berths at Central Yard and, in 1900, acquired the land at Greatham Creek that he named Graythorpe. Born in 1867, he was brought up in the locality and, after completing his education at Cambridge, joined the family business. Like his father before him, he became a generous benefactor to the people of West Hartlepool. In 1915 he presented Normanhurst House to the town for use as a hospital, set up the Hartlepools Hospital Trust and built a public swimming pool. After the First World War, Gray built a convalescent home for his workers that was later to become the Staincliffe Hotel. He died in 1923 and was succeeded by his son, a war veteran from the trenches who would face a difficult economic battle during the years of the depression.

# WORKING LIFE

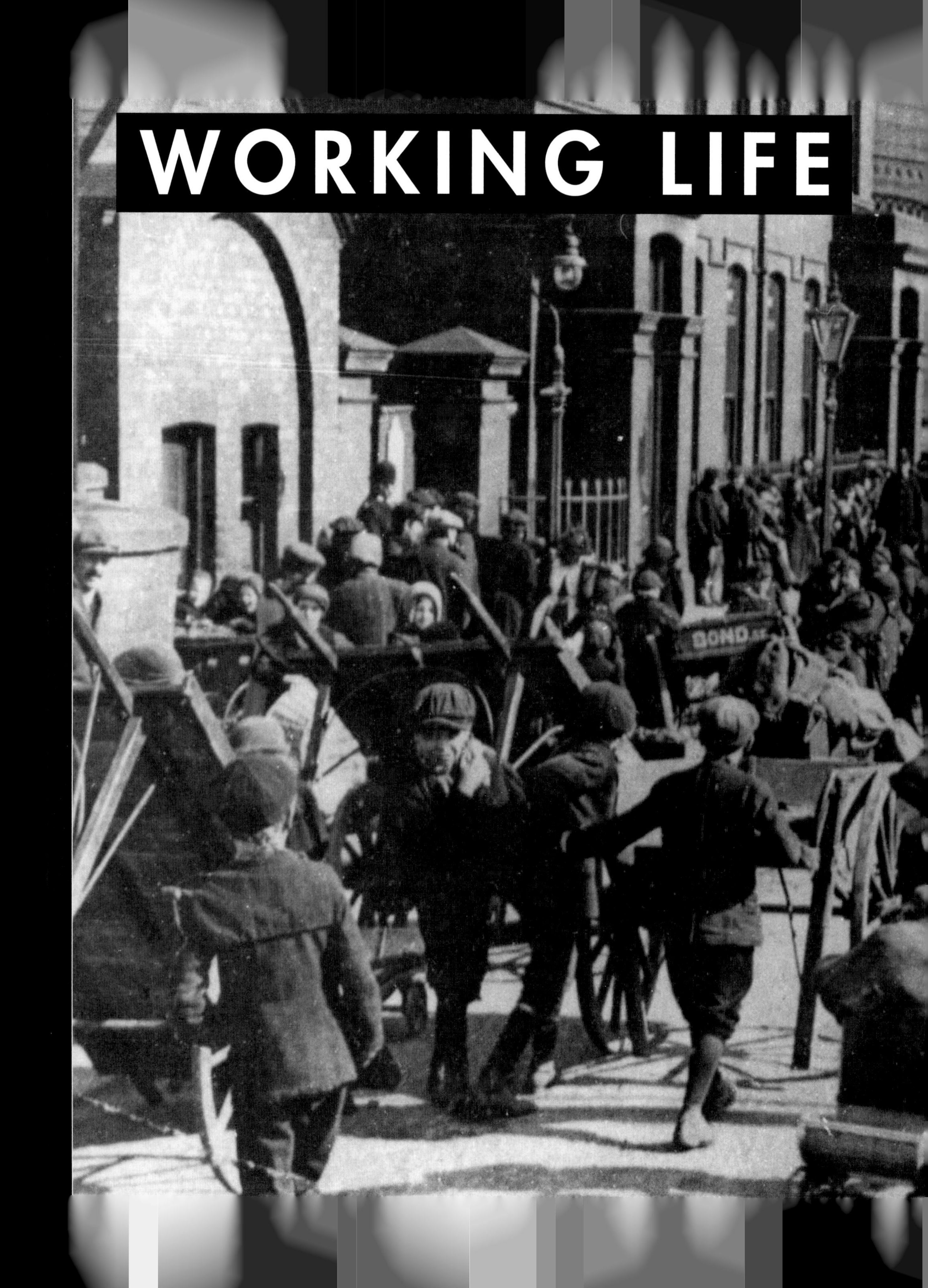

Youngsters today have it relatively easy. An awful lot is done for them and they are cosseted and protected at every time. Imagine if you were a nipper a century ago, then life would have been very different. You were expected to pull your weight. In the case of this scene that was taken literally as hordes of lads lugged heavy bags of coke about near the gas works on Middleton Road. Some heaved the sacks over their shoulders, while others commandeered prams to help them in their tasks. Priced at a tanner (6d) per bag, coke was obviously in demand on 10th March 1911 and the boys worked hard, something to which today's youth might pay heed. Still, everybody worked harder back then as there was nowhere near the same number of labour saving devices that we now enjoy. The workplace for ordinary people was something of a long grind as well. Even those employed in 'softer' jobs, such as shopworkers, had to endure long hours. That very month a bill was going through Parliament that would reduce their weekly work to a total of 60 hours. Winston Churchill, then the Home Secretary, commented that many were committed to 80 or 90 hours across a seven day week and that this was a social evil. Workers dare not object as they would lose their jobs.

**Right:** All the cares of the world were etched on the face of Mary Ferguson. Looking older than her 70 years in this 1880 photograph, she had lived through the time that had seen Britain change from a country partly dependent upon its agricultural output to one that was largely industrial by the time she reached old age. Born when Napoleon was a threat, she had seen the first railways operating, learned of a civil war in America and seen newly built large iron ships steaming out of the dockyards. All the while, she continued in her role as a gatherer of sea coal on the beach at Seaton Carew. Although of a lower quality than that brought up from the mines across the Durham coalfield, sea coal was a freely available source of fuel that she could use in her home and sell on to give her a modest living. Armed with her rake and basket, Mary went out in all weathers. Some of the coal was washed in from the sea bed, but a lot of it came from the mix of stone and coal dumped by coastal collieries. Well into the 20th century, lorries used to work the beach, collecting large loads of the fuel. What Mary would have done for such a vehicle to help her, but her time was nearly up. She passed away in 1881.

**Below:** The first fire services were often linked with insurance companies anxious to save themselves some money when

properties went up in flames. In the days long before smoke alarms and sprinkler systems, fire was a frequent occurrence in premises squashed on top of one another. Not all outbreaks were accidental, especially when an unscrupulous businessman decided that his profit margin was miserly and he could see a way to improve cash flow via a successful claim. As councils and corporations became more concerned about the welfare of the citizens they represented moves were made to regularise the provision of this emergency service. Even after the Great Fire of London in 1666 there was only a limited response, though the development of a reliable pump that supplied a continuous water jet in the early 18th century helped get things rolling more quickly. In 1824 Edinburgh became the first British city to form a properly organised brigade. However, most places continued with a mixture of community, volunteer and insurance brigades until long into the Victorian age. This was West Hartlepool's first motorised fire engine. The type of helmet the fireman is wearing became reserved for ceremonial use as it acted as a good conductor of electricity. This was not a good idea when entering a blazing building with bare wires hanging about as it led to a hair raising experience, all too literally.

**Above:** In a scene that might have been taken from Arthur Ransome's 'Swallows and Amazons', the lads were pushing off in their rowing boat to enjoy some time on the water. This is not Coniston or Windermere, but Hartlepool Bay had its own attractions for youngsters brought up by the sea. Many could handle boats from an early age, having been introduced to them by fathers who fished the sea on the sort of steam drifters we see here. They were usually quite large boats, about 80-100 feet in length, with a beam of some 20 feet. They travelled at about 10 knots, powering the 40 or 50 ton craft through the waters of the North Sea. The early ones were made of wood, but steel hulls were introduced in the late 19th century. These vessels did not need conventional sails, except for a mizzen sail that was used to steady the boat when the nets were cast. The mast acted as a crane to lift the catch ashore. Some nicknamed the drifters 'woodbines', because the long smoking funnels reminded them of a popular cigarette of the day. The main disadvantage of the steam drifters was the high running cost as they used large quantities of coal and were expensive to fit out. Their engines were also mechanically inefficient and took up a lot of space.

A woman's work is never done. This was especially true when it came to housework in the period leading up to World War One. There were very few lucky or wealthy enough to be able to afford the luxury of a vacuum cleaner. The maid carrying out the cleaning duties in a typical sitting room of the period (bottom right) was one of the first to have such a remarkable piece of equipment to help her keep her mistress's home neat and tidy. The cleaner was manufactured by Reyrolles of Hebburn, the South

carried out in fulfilling the daily domestic chores. Electrical appliances were few and far between, even for those at the top end of the social scale. Washday was an occasion for red hands and a lot of backbreaking work. Because water usually had to be heated on a fire for washing, the warm soapy water was precious and would be reused over and over, first to wash the least soiled clothing, then to wash progressively dirtier items. Housewives pounded the wash that was taking place in a dolly tub with a long pole attached to a conical base. This implement was known as a posser. They might also have rubbed the clothing on the sort of washboard that skiffle players would use in the 1950s. Having satisfied herself that the clothing was now clean, the surplus water was removed by passing the objects through a hand-cranked wringer or mangle. Then it was off to the washing line to peg everything out, with a silent prayer to the sun god that he would shine today.

Tyneside electrical engineering company. The first vacuum was a manually operated machine, invented by McGaffey of Chicago. However, it was a Briton, HG Cecil, who was the one who produced the first powered cleaner in 1901. Unfortunately, his design was overtaken by JM Spangler's rotating brush system that was sold to Hoover and became the dominant force in early electric vacuum cleaner production. The maid must have thanked her lucky stars for such a device as she no longer had to roll up the carpets and beat them outdoors on a regular basis. Her job was as part of a small team of servants that was commonplace in middle class homes. She would be accompanied by a cook and, possibly, a nanny for the large number of children that was the norm for such families. Domestic service, although not well paid, was something to which many young girls aspired. It provided a roof over their heads in clean, sanitary accommodation and got them away from the dirt and grime of work in the factories. Even so, there was still much manual work to be

**Above:** If the reader has young children, show them this view of life as it was for young Seaton Carew children on the beach in the 1890s. Some look to be as young as five, only old enough to be starting school today. But these kiddies were not destined for the classroom on this day, even though some advances in educational provision had been made by the Education Act of 1880 that made it compulsory for children to attend school until they were 10 years old. However, there were some exceptions and they could be excused attendance at times when there was great family need, especially in rural areas at harvest time. This was loosely interpreted in many quarters and used to benefit employers and parents who could use some cheap labour. These children were used to collect cockles from the sea shore. It was back-breaking work and they toiled away for long hours. The boys and girls went barefoot across the rocks, collecting the fruits of the sea that their mothers would sell from door to door and in public houses. Many of their fathers owned cobles, the flat bottomed fishing boats that were a feature of this stretch of coastline. When not in use they would be dragged up onto the beach where they would stand upright because of their particular design. The coble used to be the mainstay of the inshore fishing industry of the north-east coast. A coble was clinker-built. This means the external planks overlap each other and were fastened together with clinched copper nails. The ribs and thwarts (planks running across the width) were added after.

**Below:** William Waldon established the Lion Brewery in Stranton in 1852. The delicious spring water that flowed in abundance nearby was a good enough reason for him to base his initial business in the village. He died just two years after setting up the brewery that would ultimately become famous throughout the north-east. His widow and son inherited the business and developed it into a going concern until John Cameron became involved in the management in the 1860s. He took it over completely in 1872 and began a process of expansion by buying up smaller breweries. The brewery on Stockton Street was built in 1892 and is the oldest industrial building in the town that still serves its original purpose. It is a quite remarkable example of Victorian architecture with its imposing façade and outer gates flanked by their famous cast iron red lions. Two years after the new brewery began functioning Cameron's became a limited company. Its famous Strongarm brew was introduced in 1955. By then, millions of pints had been downed by shipbuilders and steelworkers anxious to get the dust of the day away from the backs of their throats. Cameron's was bought out by Wolverhampton and Dudley Breweries in 1972 and again, 30 years later, by Castle Eden. The photograph dates from 1967.

**Services 5 and 6. Church Street—Truro Drive—Clavering Estate**

| Stage No. | | | | | | | | | | | | | | | | | |
|---|---|---|---|---|---|---|---|---|---|---|---|---|---|---|---|---|---|
| 18 | Church Street | | | | | | | | | | | | | | | | |
| 19 | 1p | Vicarage Gardens | | | | | | | | | | | | | | | |
| 20 | 2p | 1p | St. Aidan's Church | | | | | | | | | | | | | | |
| 21 | 3p | 2p | 1p | Windermere Road | | | | | | | | | | | | | |
| 22 | 4p | 3p | 2p | 1p | Queensland Road | | | | | | | | | | | | |
| 23 | 4p | 4p | 3p | 2p | 1p | Fens Hotel | | | | | | | | | | | |
| 24 | 4p | 4p | 4p | 3p | 2p | 1p | Rossmere School | | | | | | | | | | |
| 25 | 5p | 4p | 4p | 4p | 3p | 2p | 1p | Tynebrooke Avenue | | | | | | | | | |
| 26 | 5p | 5p | 4p | 4p | 4p | 3p | 2p | 1p | Tristram Avenue | | | | | | | | |
| 27 | 6p | 5p | 5p | 4p | 4p | 4p | 3p | 2p | 1p | St. Aidan's Church | | | | | | | |
| 28 | 6p | 6p | 5p | 5p | 4p | 4p | 4p | 3p | 2p | 1p | Park Road | | | | | | |
| 29 | 7p | 6p | 6p | 5p | 5p | 4p | 4p | 4p | 3p | 2p | 1p | Odeon Cinema | | | | | |
| 30 | 7p | 7p | 6p | 6p | 5p | 5p | 4p | 4p | 4p | 3p | 2p | 1p | Raby Gardens | | | | |
| 31 | 8p | 7p | 7p | 6p | 6p | 5p | 5p | 4p | 4p | 4p | 3p | 2p | 1p | Warren Road | | | |
| 32 | 8p | 8p | 7p | 7p | 6p | 6p | 5p | 5p | 4p | 4p | 4p | 3p | 2p | 1p | Bruntoft Avenue | | |
| 33 | 8p | 8p | 8p | 7p | 7p | 6p | 6p | 5p | 5p | 4p | 4p | 4p | 3p | 2p | 1p | Easington Road Cross Rds. | |
| 34 | 9p | 8p | 8p | 8p | 7p | 7p | 6p | 6p | 5p | 5p | 4p | 4p | 4p | 3p | 2p | 1p | Bellasis Way |

**Additional fares on special journeys:—**

**Remploy Special:** Church Street to Trading Estate 3p; Tristram Avenue to Trading Estate 4p; Tynebrooke Avenue to Trading Estate 4p; Rossmere School to Trading Estate 5p; Fens Hotel to Trading Estate 5p

**School Special:** Odeon to St. Bede's R. C. School 3p; Holdforth Road to St. Bede's R.C. School 4p

It is a long time since we saw 'clippies' on our buses. The conductresses, who were so nicknamed as they originally clipped off a corner of the ticket they had issued earlier, were a common sight on public transport in the postwar era. Although not practised everywhere, it was quite common to sell a ticket to a passenger and later in the journey check that the customer had not travelled beyond his allotted stage. From time to time inspectors would board the bus and check the clippie's work and do a further round on both decks to ensure that everything was tickety-boo, as you might say. Drivers and conductresses made up a good team, working together for the benefit of the general public. Regular commuters and shoppers did not really get to know the man behind the wheel as he was marooned in his cab, but the clippie became something of an old friend. The elderly were helped on board and children often regarded her as a surrogate auntie as she took an interest in their school projects and toys they carried. Budding Lotharios could get a little cheeky, with remarks such as, 'How far can I go for a tanner, pet?' but she took it in good stead and usually had a witty rejoinder to put them in their place. Of course, there were the odd ones who had an evil streak. They would watch someone running towards the bus stop and wait until he was just a few yards away before ringing the bell that signalled the driver to move off. Those of us approaching middle age and beyond will remember D-Day. This was not the one from 1944, but the day when the cash in our pockets was changed forever. On 15th February 1971, we went decimal. Bobs, tanners and even pennies became obsolete. No more florins or half crowns as everything altered to what was first known as 'new pence'. Shops, pubs and garages listed prices in both the old and decimal forms as people tried to come to terms with the pint of beer that used to be 2s 4d but was now 12p. Accusations of profiteering flew thick and fast as prices were, of course, always rounded up and it was said that we would never get used to this foreign, continental idea of working in tens and hundreds. But we did. Children, especially, made the changeover quite smoothly and their parents soon followed suit. The ticket rolls pictured were used on the Ultimate ticket machine that was carried by all conductors from August 1971 onwards. The fare table was one of the first amended ones to be published in time for the day we went decimal and Lsd disappeared into the history books.

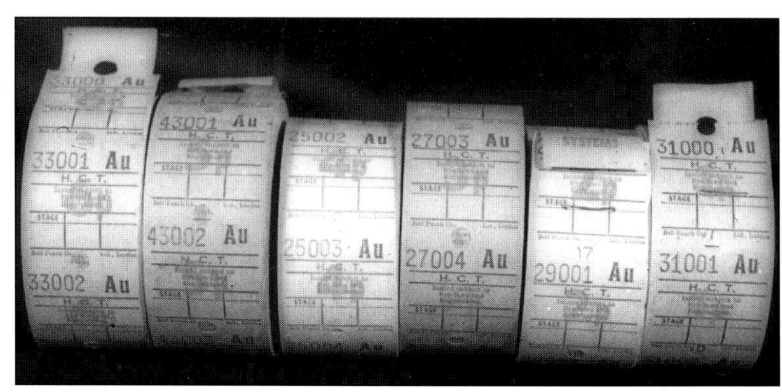

SHOP AT BINNS
2
CHURCH STREET

# Yuill Homes - Built on Firm Foundations

For over 80 years, the Yuill Homes name has been synonymous with innovation beyond expectation in house building throughout the North East of England. From the very beginning the Hartlepool firm has aimed not just to accommodate the desires of the day, but to plan for those of tomorrow – and always with the utmost respect for the local environment. Hence its nationally-acclaimed, breathtaking reinvention of listed landmark buildings, such as Princess Mary Court and Lanesborough Court in Newcastle, designed with forethought and sensitivity not only to maintain but to enhance the essential character of the original buildings and their surroundings. And it has lavished as much care and attention to detail on its latest award-winning regeneration development at Longbenton, Newcastle. Where again, the Vermont, its award-winning best starter home, never fails to surprise and delight, with two bedrooms and two en-suite bathrooms.

Cecil M Yuill Limited was founded in 1927 by Cecil Mortley Yuill who was then 19 years old. Five years later he sold his first two houses – numbers 20 and 22 Marlborough Street, Hartlepool - for £324 each. In the following decades tens of thousands of new Yuill homes would be built in the area.

Cecil Mortley Yuill was born in West Hartlepool in June 1907. In 1920, at the age of 13, he began working for his grandfather, a master plasterer, who had started in business as a jobbing builder and chimney sweep in the 1890s. Cecil was equipped with only a handcart and a pair of ladders, but he had an unquenchable appetite for hard work and a driving ambition to improve his lot.

After receiving training from his grandfather Cecil became a bricklayer in a jobbing partnership with him, earning six shillings a week. He supplemented his income by playing a

***Top left:** Founder Cecil Yuill. **Below:** Cecil Yuill (second from the left) and dance band colleagues pictured in the 1920s.*

trumpet in a Hartlepool dance band on three nights each week, often playing until midnight before starting work the next day at 4am. The savings his two jobs enabled him to make gave him the capital to start up his own building business.

Cecil's youthful life with his grandfather lasted seven years until he decided to set up on his own.

Even in those dark and difficult days it was clear to all around him that Cecil had what it took to succeed: driving ambition, an abundance of energy and the desire to improve by quickly learning new skills.

In the years leading up to the Second World War, Cecil Yuill expanded his business, building houses in both the private and public sectors in his home town of Hartlepool. Being a small builder in the 1920s was not an easy task, but by 1932 Cecil was building his first houses in Marlborough Street, Hartlepool. His first contract for 150 council houses came five years later.

Under pressure from the War Office, the business became a limited company (Cecil M Yuill Ltd) in 1940. During the war Cecil, together with the volunteer squad he had recruited, worked each Monday to Thursday repairing bomb damage for the London Borough of Wandsworth. From Friday to Sunday he spent building fortifications for the Admiralty along the north-east coast.

After the war the company grew to become one of the North East's principal housing companies. In 1945 the turnover was £43,868. By 1952 it had risen to £321,000, principally from contract work. Within three years that turnover had doubled, and Cecil Yuill's strategic guidance saw the company acquire significant land purchases in the fifties and sixties. This meant the company focused its attention and achieved its biggest success building private houses for homebuyers in the north-east.

By 1960 the annual turnover had reached almost £800,000. Significant achievements were the building of Brierton Modern School, costing £350,000, the construction of 500 Unity houses and, most prestigious of all, the building of 208 three-storey flats in Sunderland.

***Top left:*** *The Cecil M Yuill original premises pictured in 1940.* ***Left:*** *An old company bus.* ***Below:*** *C M Yuill staff of 1945.*

Three Bedroom Detached
£3,100
The Grosvenor

Three Bedroom
Semi-Detached £2,490
The Stranton

# WHAT WE BUILD

*—Choice of Twelve Basic Designs—*

THESE ARE JUST A FEW OF THE HOUSES C. M. Yuill are building on eight major sites in the Tees-side area. Customers are offered 12 basic designs for dwellings varying in basic price from £2,300 to £7,000. All houses are built to a very high specification and all carry the ten year NHBRC guarantee. Under this new 10 year protection scheme C. M. YUILL LTD. agrees during the first 2 years to put right at the company's expense, any structural or non structural defects arising from failure to comply with the NHBRC specifications. From the second to the tenth year the council undertakes to cover the house against any major damage due to latent structural defects.

Inspection is of a very high standard and every member builder is required to allow the council free access to all sites to inspect houses periodically while being built.

Over 3,300 homes are scheduled to be built by the company and of these, 650 will be completed this year.

The largest building site is at **West Hartlepool**, where 1,740 homes are being built at the **Fens Estate.**

Close by at **Seaton Carew,** half of the 220 scheduled houses are already occupied.

At **Durham,** on a new site two miles from the centre, 650 houses are planned, while at **South Park, West Hartlepool,** 100 houses have yet to be built.

**Mowden Park, Darlington** offers a truly picturesque site where a large portion of natural aspect has been retained, and grass and trees combine to avoid the "estate" look.

Detached houses and bungalows which are being built at **Peterlee** should be completed this year.

Other sites are at **Kirkleatham Lane, Redcar,** and the **Orchard Estate Eaglescliffe,** where the second stage of development has started on the east side of Durham Lane.

"THE PARKSTON"
Three Bedrooms
£2,750

"THE STAMFORD"
Three Bedroom Semi-Detached £2,300

"THE NAIRN"
Two Bedroom Detached Bungalow
£3,075

"THE KENMORE"
Two/Three Bedroom
Semi £2,490

"THE FYLINGDALE"
Three Bedroom Detached, Garage, French Window to Rear, Breakfast Nook to Kitchen and Fitted Wardrobes in Two Main Bedrooms £3,350

"THE ABBEY"
Three Bedroom
Semi-Detached £2,770

By 1968 the Firm's 64,000 square feet modern factory employed 120 operatives, whilst the company also had 180 staff members and 1,150 workers on its 15 sites.

In 1969, after 43 years in business, the company moved into purpose-built headquarters at Loyalty Road in Hartlepool, where it has remained ever since. By then Cecil Yuill was a leading member of the local Master Builders' Association, and the Northern Counties Regional Federation Building Trades Employers, active in London as well as the North East.

In 1972, after 45 years service, Cecil Yuill officially retired on his 65th birthday. During his time at the helm he had presided over remarkable changes; by then turnover was some £4 million and the once tiny business now had over 1,000 workers. Cecil M Yuill Limited had become one of the most important construction companies, as well as one of the largest employers, in the region.

After Cecil Yuill's retirement in 1972, the company was grateful to retain his services as a consultant. The business continued its growth to become one of the largest providers of private homes in the North East. In 1995, after seven decades of quality building for the local community, over one fifth of all homes in Hartlepool and almost 30,000 homes throughout the North East had been built by the Yuill Homes.

Throston and G R Howe were acquired in 1973 to add building services to the company's established reputation for building expertise.

It was a well-earned reward when, in 1989, Yuill won the building industry's highest accolade - the National Housing Design Award - for an outstanding development at Collingwood Court, Morpeth, Northumberland.

Yuill Homes is a developer of high quality, traditionally built private housing, with a long established reputation in its North East territory. Its product range includes starter homes, three and four bedroom family homes through to five bedroom executive properties, luxury apartments and town houses.

The design of the houses and the site and street layouts are produced by an experienced team of in-house architects and designers, often supplemented by nationally renowned architects, resulting in a set of house ranges with distinctive designs and styles which are unique to the Yuill name.

***Top left:*** *A selection of houses built by Yuill in the 1960s.* ***Above:*** *An early Yuill exhibition.* ***Left:*** *The company's first head office.*

Yuill sells its product on each development, using its own highly-trained and experienced sales negotiators and makes full use of branded sales and showhouse areas to enhance and display the product.

However, even the most brilliant management needs a committed workforce in order to succeed.

Yuill workers are valued and well treated and repay the company with long service. One company bricklayer, who served his time during the war repairing bomb-damaged houses with Cecil Yuill himself, stayed with the firm until he finally stepped down in 1994. At least five of the Site Management team were Yuill apprentices who have been developed into their current role.

The company's reputation for quality and innovation was built on the competence and expertise, skills and, just as importantly, the enthusiasm and commitment of its employees.

The organisation places a huge emphasis on staff training and development and justly rewards employees for their positive input.

Ever since the firm was founded it has produced 'home grown' tradesmen through apprenticeship schemes. Even during the recession of the 1980s when most house builders stopped such training one in ten of Yuill's workforce were apprentices.

The company was one of the first house builders to be recognised as an Investor in People, a status that was achieved in 1995.

Meanwhile step inside any Yuill home and the firm's key priorities are immediately apparent: space, light, flexibility, contemporary comfort, and individual choice. The company likes to bring that extra special something - the 'wow' factor - to its homes, regardless of price. It could take the shape of sunlit mezzanine bedrooms, fully equipped en-suite bathrooms or even a choice of entertainment suites. The firm likes to think it has thought of all the little things which can turn a house into every buyer's very own dream home. Yuill ideas and designs have earned it an impressive collection of awards, but most importantly they have earned the firm an impressive number of lifelong buyers.

***Top left:*** *A staff Christmas party in the 1960s, Mr and Mrs Cecil Yuill can be seen centre right.* ***Left and below:*** *The Yuill family examine contents of a time capsule buried under Cecil House in 1969.*

In 2006 the Yuill family ended its long connection with the firm when it was acquired by Taggart Holdings.

Founded in 1989 by brothers John and Michael Taggart, their company has grown from a Northern Ireland-based house builder to a vibrant and dynamic international property development company, with offices in Ireland, the UK, Eastern Europe and the USA.

Taggart Holdings has offices in Belfast, Derry and Manchester to service its UK and Ireland operations. In addition the group has representative offices in Europe and Florida to source potential opportunities in Central and Eastern Europe and in the United States.

Recent successes include recognition for Taggart's Brooke Hall development as Best Residential Development in Northern Ireland at the 2006 Irish Property Awards. The company also picked up another NHBC Pride in the Job quality award for its Forthill development.

Taggart Holdings property remit extends to all areas of development. Its current property portfolio includes both residential and commercial properties in Ireland, UK, mainland Europe, New Zealand and Eastern Europe, with a combined land bank valued in excess of £500 million

***Above:*** *The opening of Greenways Estate in Spennymoor.* ***Right:*** *Apprentices pictured in the 1970s.* ***Below:*** *The Yuill family, front row left to right: Phillip, Patricia (Wilson nee Yuill), Hilda, Cecil and Peter, pictured with the Hartlepool United players and staff at the opening (by Cecil Yuill) of the Cecil M Yuill Diamond Jubilee Stand in 1987.*

Yuill Homes expertise however continues to focus on the North East region and its credentials cover an extensive portfolio of high profile, award-winning or just plain good quality housing developments across a broad spectrum of projects – from new build to the renovation of historic buildings and the revitalisation of redundant brown field sites. The result is an unrivalled understanding of the economic pressures and changing profile of the area.

Cecil M Yuill died in August 1992 at the age of 85; he was widely recognised as the leader in his field.

In celebration of his life the Cecil M Yuill Foundation was formed to introduce three permanent educational initiatives into the area. The first of these was the Cecil M Yuill Chair of Construction at the University of Teesside and its School of Science and Technology. The second, the provision of up to four financial awards to students at the University who have demonstrated significant self-motivation and progress throughout their courses. The third initiative was to reward individuals who have achieved academic excellence despite disadvantaged personal circumstances. The charitable foundation's principal objective, however, is simply assisting young people in realising their true potential as individuals both at University and in their lives.

Cecil himself was always regarded by all who came into contact with him as a 'man of the people' with the unique ability to demonstrate how self-improvement could be achieved. Few men knew better what could be achieved with hard work and application. The 13-year-old jobbing builder who had once pushed a handcart around the streets of Hartlepool in the 1920s could easily have achieved nothing in life; instead his legacy includes not merely bricks and mortar but something more valuable still – a better chance for young people to build lives as well as houses.

Most recently Yuill Homes has been particularly pleased to be building homes in Hartlepool as part of the regeneration of the town.

The scheme was voted for by local residents. Through extensive consultation, residents stated that they wanted older homes in the development area to be replaced by new build housing.

After a competitive tendering process Yuill Homes was identified as the preferred developer of the new high quality housing in the New Deal for Communities Community Housing Plan area.

As a result 347 properties on two sites are affected by the demolition and will be replaced by new houses built by Yuill Homes.

Today, although leading the field in new technologies and innovative thinking, Yuill Homes never forgets its own foundations. The firm now builds over 300 houses each year with some 250 employees. Cecil Yuill once remarked that the people of the North East had been good to Yuill's and that Yuill's should never forget to be good to them in return. The promise has been taken to heart by the company. Now in the 21st century, as part of Taggart Holdings, Yuill Homes continues to move forward with confidence – in both itself and in the region which is its home.

***Above:*** *One of Yuill's award-winning projects, Queensbury at Longbenton, won Best Partnership Development and Best Starter Home for the Vermont.* ***Below:*** *The Yuill Group's head office, Cecil House, Loyalty Road, Hartlepool.*

# *Hartlepool Water - Supplying Quality Water Since 1846*

Based at 3 Lancaster Road, Hartlepool Water's company history goes back to the early years of Queen Victoria's reign. Hartlepool Gas and Water Company was formed in 1846. The original company, as its name suggests, also supplied gas. Local businessmen appreciated that pure water would promote the health and comfort of the town's 10,000 inhabitants.

The Hartlepool Gas and Water Company's first source of water was a single-cylinder steam engine pump which delivered 40,000 litres of water an hour from a site in Brougham Terrace behind the present Hartlepool Water offices.

In those early days the average consumption of water was less than 20 litres a head a day, at a cost of 1p a cubic metre. Around six miles of main were needed to supply the Headland, West Hartlepool and Seaton Carew.

The first town showroom was opened in Church Street in 1901. The water supply was extended to Hart in 1903 and land was bought at Howbeck for the sinking of more boreholes. The following year Crookfoot reservoir was formally opened.

New premises were needed, and offices were taken in Lancaster Road. (The current offices were built on the same site in the 1970s.) The company's property suffered extensive damage when Hartlepool was bombed in the First World War. The waterworks were hit, but quick repairs made it possible to keep the supply going. Seven employees were wounded, however, and one killed. The government paid £7,500 for bomb damage.

During the Second World War shortage of men was more of a problem. Though gas and water mains were damaged on 19 occasions, the supply was never cut off.

Today the company successfully meets the most stringent health requirements, supplying pure and wholesome water to 90,000 inhabitants in the town.

***Top left:*** *Monitoring flows into supply at Dalton Piercy site, 1960.* ***Above:*** *Water examination in the late 1950s.* ***Left:*** *An early view inside the boiler room.* ***Below:*** *Early examination of pump connections.*

The company has 19 boreholes on 11 sites stretching from near Darlington to Dalton Piercy. It pumps up to three million litres of water an hour. The cost of metered water is now between 58p and 90p per cubic metre, one of the lowest charges in the country. The average consumption now is around 150 litres a head each day, supplied through 580km of water mains. A free meter option was offered to householders in 1998. Today around 17% of homes have a water meter.

Global warming, which means less rain, is a big concern to the company. In addition, the Environment Act 1995 imposed on water companies a new legal duty to promote the efficient use of water by customers. Staff therefore measure very accurately the lowest flow at night into an area. After allowing for customers' night use, the rest is accounted for as leakage. Such tests mean the company can concentrate on looking for leaks where leakage is highest.

In the 1990s Hartlepool Water Company became Hartlepool Water PLC; it remained an independent company quoted on the Stock Market until 1997 when Anglian Water bought the business for around £18m.

Since 1997 the business has been successful in developing competition locally both with the retention of some important business customers and through offering value added services to customers.

The Business Development Section offers water supply, water treatment, wastewater treatment and support services. Small-business-style customer care is backed by the technical capability and financial muscle of a large parent.

Meeting its water quality obligations, however, remains the company's number one priority.

The standards to which the company works are laid down in legislation is The Water Supply (Water Quality) Regulations 2000.

Hartlepool Water checks the water supplies for a range of chemical and microbiological parameters as it travels from the borehole sources, through treatment and storage, to customer taps. Sampling takes place throughout the year to ensure that it delivers safe and acceptable water supplies.

Today Hartlepool Water aims to maintain high levels of customer satisfaction by investing £1 million each year. That investment is in two key areas: maintaining the high service levels to customers, and maintaining security of service. This balances investment with the lowest price limits necessary to maintain services, comply with legal requirements, and deliver the high services, which the company believes its customers want. Of the 25 water companies in England and Wales, Hartlepool Water will remain the fifth cheapest by 2010.

***Top left:*** *Triple Expansion engine in the 1930s.* ***Top right:*** *Spillway construction at Crookfoot Reservoir.* ***Left:*** *Laying water mains in the 1960s.* ***Above:*** *Well drilling at Naisberry in the 1960s.*

# F.Shotton Ltd

## A Family Firm Going from Strength to Strength

Some names come and go in just a few years. Businesses popular with previous generations of satisfied customers simply cease to exist. Happily, there remain some examples of business names which do last down the decades, ensuring that customers who were pleased with the service they got years earlier can return and be satisfied all over again.

The amazing growth of Shottons' Furniture Store from a small electrical shop to a large ultra modern showroom in York Road fitted with the very latest furniture from all around the world has been the result of three things: customer service which is second to none, keen pricing and a loyal staff, many of whom have been with the firm since leaving school.

Frank and May Shotton, joint founders of the firm officially titled F Shotton Ltd, started out in business in Belk Street in 1959 at premises previously known as the 'Kit Kat Café'. There they sold every type of electrical appliance from the small single unit shop. With increasing national affluence and the swinging sixties just ahead it was a good time to start a new enterprise.

Three sons, Keith, Gerald and Roger, soon joined the business.

By the mid-1960s Shottons had bought an old warehouse next door in Raby Road and began selling furniture and carpets. Keith Shotton, the eldest of the three sons, took main responsibility for sourcing quality furniture from suppliers such as Guy Rogers, Vono and Bridgecraft.

Tony, a fourth son, joined the business in the late 1960s after serving in the Army for nine years. The business continued to grow, and in 1971 a major extension was built which saw a second floor added to the existing showroom. Two years later a further store was opened in Stockton, premises which had previously been the gas showroom in Norton Road.

In 1974 Clive Shotton, the fifth and youngest of Frank and May's sons, joined the family firm.

***Above:*** *Founders, Frank and May Shotton.* ***Below left and below:*** *Two views of the F Shotton showroom on Raby Road in the 1960s.*

With new impetus a warehouse in York Road Hartlepool, which had already been in use for some time by Shottons, was converted into a bedroom showroom, whilst another 10,000 sq ft warehouse was bought nearby.

Inspired by his parents' example, Roger Shotton left the business in 1977 to branch out with his own kitchen centre. He was soon followed by Keith and Tony who opened the Stockton store as their own kitchen centre.

Gerald left in 1982, leaving just the youngest son Clive in the business.

Today Clive Shotton runs the business with the help of his wife Sandra, who has herself worked for Shottons since 1977 running the administration side of the business.

Frank and May Shotton took an active part in the business all their lives.

In May 2002, however, May sadly passed away aged 88. Frank never seemed to get over the loss; they had been married for almost 64 years although he still worked six days a week, famously 'first through the door and last to leave'. Frank Shotton died in 2005 at the age of 85.

Shottons has become a name for top quality furniture and carpets in Hartlepool and the North East. The firm has become the largest furniture business in Hartlepool offering quality furniture to the public.

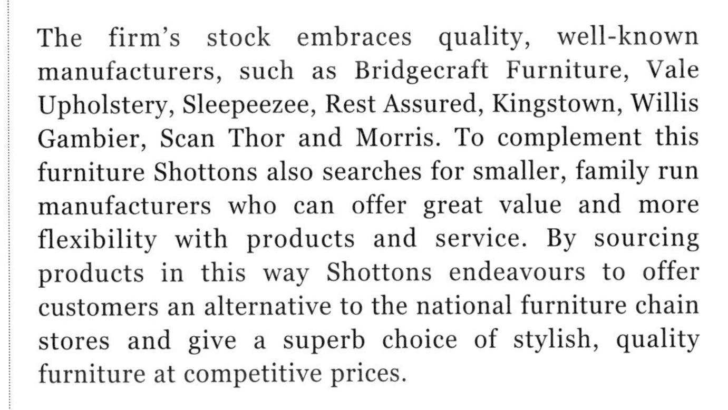

The firm's stock embraces quality, well-known manufacturers, such as Bridgecraft Furniture, Vale Upholstery, Sleepeezee, Rest Assured, Kingstown, Willis Gambier, Scan Thor and Morris. To complement this furniture Shottons also searches for smaller, family run manufacturers who can offer great value and more flexibility with products and service. By sourcing products in this way Shottons endeavours to offer customers an alternative to the national furniture chain stores and give a superb choice of stylish, quality furniture at competitive prices.

In 2006 the firm demolished its bedroom centre in York Road and built a brand new store, which linked up to the warehouse creating a grand total of 20,000 sq ft with customer parking for some 30 cars at a time. Meanwhile the firm still retains its original Raby Road store where Frank and May Shotton began their business so many years ago.

***Top left**: Shotton's new walk around showroom after the extension in 1971. **Above left and below**: Clive Shotton, who with his wife, Sandra, runs the new Shottons showroom in York Road, pictured below.*

# Greylin Engineering - Engineering Excellence

Greylin Engineering Ltd celebrated 30 years in business in 2006 It was on 30th April 1976 that the company was set up by Lawrence Inman. A former ICI employee, he obtained premises at Graythorpe which had formerly been an RAF camp. There the company began to establish itself in precision and general engineering, serving the chemical, steelmaking, offshore, brewing, textile and electrical industries.

The company had grown sufficiently by the early 1980s to need new premises, and in 1983 a move was made to Hartlepool's Tofts Farm Industrial Estate. Lawrence's son Ken was already well established in the firm, having joined it in 1977, and in 1984 Richard Inman, grandson of the founder, also arrived.

In the early nineties, with Ken Inman now the Managing Director, the company was anxious to demonstrate its commitment to quality. In 1990 it received a fortuitous letter from Hartlepool Enterprise Agency, giving information about a one-day seminar entitled, 'Introducing Quality Standards. The company was represented on the course and made good use of the information on offer. It also contacted and received valuable help from the Department of Trade and Industry. Advice was also taken from consultants Touche Ross of Newcastle.

Standards make an enormous and positive contribution to most aspects of our lives. More importantly for businesses, having nationally recognised standards creates confidence in potential clients, many of whom will not deal with suppliers whose standards are not certified.

Standards ensure desirable characteristics of products and services such as quality, environmental friendliness, safety, reliability, efficiency and interchangeability - and at an economical cost.

When products and services meet customers' expectations, they tend to take this for granted and be unaware of the role of standards. However, when standards are absent everyone soon

**Top left:** *Founder, Lawrence Inman.* **Above:** *Where it all began, Greylin's original premises at Graythorpe.* **Left:** *Managing Director Ken Inman is presented with the BS 5750 Certificate in April 1992.* **Below:** *At work inside Greylin.*

notices. Customers quickly complain if products turn out to be of poor quality, do not fit, are incompatible with equipment that they already have, or are unreliable or dangerous.
When products, systems, machinery and devices work well and safely, it is often because they meet standards. Having recognised standards is vital for industry.

As far back as the 1970s many major organisations published their own quality management standards (eg Ford's Q101 and the Ministry of Defence's 05-20 series.). Those standards introduced the idea that confidence in a product could be gained from an approved quality management system and quality manuals. By the late 1970s it was decided that, for the first time, there would be a national standard on what constituted a quality system. BS5750 was developed and become the gold standard to which firms could aspire.

Though onerous to achieve, BS 5750 became Greylin Engineering's aim and the whole workforce made every effort to achieve it quickly.

Councillor Bob Barnfather, Chairman of the Council's economic development committee, was pleased to be able to present part 2 of the BS 5750 certificate to Greylin Engineering Ltd in April 1992. This was the year that saw the birth of the open European market, which the company entered with an accredited indication of its ability in forward thinking, which had caused it to apply it in the first place, and in quality, which enabled its staff to achieve it.

The company also achieved ISO 9002. Its customers include Corus, British Energy, Cleveland Potash, Wilton Engineering Services and many other well-known companies. They attribute their success to taking the trouble to match components exactly to customer requirements.

In recent years, as three key employees approached retirement age, which threatened to leave the firm with a shortage of skilled labour, the firm set up its own apprentice-training department. The course takes four years to complete. Since then the scheme has trained six tradesmen with another still in the second year of training.

Serving local industry, the company has gained many new customers in the last ten years.

Never a firm to rest on its laurels, Greylin is constantly upgrading its machinery and its procedures. Four CNC (computer controlled) machines have been introduced for turning and milling to close tolerances of just five microns.

Now in the 21st Century Greylin Engineering Ltd is looking forward to further qualifications and even more satisfied customers.

***Top left:*** *Ken Inman (right) and son Richard alongside one of the four CNC machines introduced for turning and milling.* ***Centre:*** *A selection of products manufactured by Greylin Engineering.* ***Below:*** *Ken and Richard with part of the company's modern fleet (also inset).*

# *tbi - Legal Evolution*

Sooner or later most of us will need a solicitor. And who better to choose than a firm which has stood the test of time? tbi – Tilly Bailey & Irvine - is one of the North East's leading full service legal practices. Today the firm has offices in York Chambers,York Road, Hartlepool, as well as Stockton-on-Tees, Wynyard Park and Barnard Castle.

The firm's story began in the Victorian era. At the turn of the 20th century a legal partnership, Turnbull & Tilly, practised in Hartlepool. They were Notaries Public dealing with shipmasters' claims and were based in the same office at 13, Church Street in which Edward Turnbull had originally started his practice in 1841.

The original Mr Tilly took his eldest son into the partnership and the firm continued until Tilly senior's death in 1932. The firm was then expanded by amalgamation with two other local firms. As Temperley, Tilly & Hayward, it moved to larger offices in Church Street, opposite Turnbull's first premises.

In 1949 Mr JB Irvine, the son of a West Hartlepool timber merchant, entered into partnership with FWJ Webb. Mr Webb, had been practising with Edward Fryer, a firm established in 1897. As Fryer, Webb & Irvine, the new partnership continued until 1955 when it amalgamated with Harry Bailey & Son, becoming Webb, Bailey & Irvine. The latter practice worked in association with Temperley, Tilly & Hayward amalgamating in 1969, to form the present firm.

Looking back it seems quite remarkable that the present firm's predecessors operated with just two partners and a small supporting staff. Now the firm has no fewer than fifteen partners and 140 staff including other solicitors and executives, plus secretaries, support staff, and the resource of lawyers using the very latest technology for the benefit of clients.

Over many years tbi has evolved to meet the changing needs of clients. In the early days, much of

Over the preceding two years tbi's business law office more than doubled its workload. The team increased to a total of 26 staff, including 15 specialist lawyers, in the key business law areas of corporate transactions, commercial property, intellectual property and IT, employment, commercial dispute resolution and commercial contracts. In fact the firm boasts the only dedicated specialist IP and IT team in the Tees Valley.

The team at tbi is committed to providing high quality support to its clients. The depth and breadth of experience at tbi allows it to cater for all client needs.

John Hall became Managing Partner in September 2007 having joined tbi in 1976, where he completed his articles, qualifying as a solicitor the same year. He became head of the Personal Injury Department and was appointed a Partner after just two year's service.

***Far left:*** *Tobias Harry Tilly senior.* ***Left:*** *Harry Bailey.* ***Below:*** *Managing Partner John Hall, 2008.*

its expertise was in the traditional north-eastern industries of coal, shipping and steel. Today, it is geared to the fast-changing personal and business environment of the 21st century.

The firm offers a full investment management and stockbroking service. The Investment Department is staffed by experienced investment management personnel, and supervised by a partner authorised by the Solicitors Regulatory Authority to deal in securities and portfolios.

The practice places great emphasis on the traditional values of courtesy, integrity and friendliness. It combines this with very modern offices and the technology to provide clients with a service which is swift, cost-effective and personal.

tbi prides itself on being responsive to client needs and takes a progressive and forward thinking approach. In September 2005 it became a Limited Liability Partnership. The success and growth of the business law office at Stockton led to tbi securing new premises on the prestigious 700-acre Wynyard Park business development. The business law team moved in to the Evolution suites at Wynyard Park in autumn 2007.

# Trust and Reliability - WA Smith Insurance Brokers

In 1897, William Abbey Smith and his elder brother Charles Edward Smith started the partnership of Smith Bros & Co in West Hartlepool, to undertake marine surveying, steamship and insurance broking. It was not long before the brothers became ship owners themselves, acquiring three ships which were built locally in the William Gray Shipyard.

The brothers' partnership ended in 1907 and William Abbey Smith moved from the first offices at Royal Chambers in Church Street to trade as a 'Steamship and Insurance Broker' in new premises at 3 Stockton Street, from where the business would be conducted for the next 60 years.

***Top:*** *WA Smith 1863-1950.* ***Right:*** *James Edmund Smith, 1904-1994.* ***Below inset:*** *The 'Knaresbro' at 4,645 tons and 235 feet in length it was the largest of the three ships owned by the firm.* ***Below:*** *Stockton Street, West Hartlepool, in the 1950s.*

In 1926, James Edmund Smith, son of the founder, joined the business and would work there until a short time before his death in 1994. He was joined in the business in 1963 by his two sons, the current directors, Michael and Philip Smith.

At that time West Hartlepool's main shopping area was Musgrave Street, Lynn Street and Church Street. The firm's premises were in Stockton Street, on the corner of Upper Church Street. It was at those old-fashioned first floor offices that Mike and Phil first entered the world of insurance.

The firm moved from Stockton Street to York Road in 1967, and to its present offices on the corner of Victoria Road in 1981. Along with their father the brothers celebrated the 75th anniversary of the business in 1972.

By 1977 the firm had grown to such an extent that computerisation was necessary. Installation of an IBM computer was a major achievement for Smiths, which became the first provincial broking business to

computerise. The firm would grow to become one of the largest of its type in the North East, with clients from across the whole of the UK

In 1996 the firm was named as 'Broker of the Year' in a contest run by the industry. "I believe that the confidence and respect of the insurers we deal with is very important for our clients," comments Mike Smith. "However, our impartiality in the selection of the most suitable insurer is uncompromising. This duty to clients is the cornerstone of good broking practice and the firm is not afraid to fight the client's corner when required, to ensure that the insurer sticks to its side of the bargain."

Phil Smith has been a member of the Chartered Insurance Institute since 1964. He gained his Associateship Diploma in 1969 and the status of Chartered Insurance Practitioner (now Chartered Insurance Broker) in 1995. He was elected as

President of the Middlesbrough Insurance Institute in 1981 and again in 1997. The latter was in recognition of the happy coincidence that WA Smith Insurance Brokers shared its centenary with the Chartered Insurance Institute and also the 75th anniversary of the Middlesbrough Institute – and, as one wag pointed out, "Smithy's 50th birthday as well!"

Looking back over his career, Phil says, "We have been very fortunate in having excellent, loyal staff. For example, Sue Pritchard, who completed 25 years with the firm in 2007 and was appointed as a director in 1999, is a key member of the team. Despite the latest technology, clients still receive a personal and friendly service. Conducting business on the basis of mutual confidence means that over the years, people become friends as well as valued clients so it is not unusual for two or three generations of the same family to be insured here. I would like to thank those many, many long standing clients who it has been a real pleasure to serve over so many years."

'We work hard,' says Mike, 'but we always try to give an honest and straightforward service without any gimmicks. We have seen many local insurance firms come and go down the years and it is a source of satisfaction to see the progress we have made in that time.'

As to the future, the fourth generation is now in place, with Phil's son Martin joining the family business in 2003. The firm can compete with anyone on experience and technical expertise and is in the best position to obtain quality cover and value for money on behalf of clients. The latest computer technology ensures that the firm is able to offer the very cheapest quotes. Sound advice and personal service has been their hallmark for generations, so individuals and the business community can have every confidence in dealing with WA Smith Insurance Brokers Ltd, a

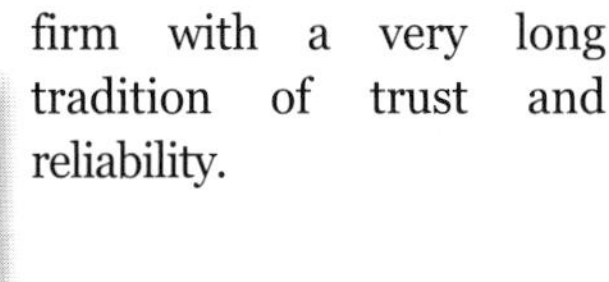
firm with a very long tradition of trust and reliability.

***Top left:*** *Receiving the Broker of the Year Award in 1996.* ***Far left:*** *Phil Smith is elected as President of the Middlesbrough Insurance Institute.* ***Above:*** *W A Smith share their centenary with the Chartered Insurance Institute in 1997.* ***Left:*** *Celebrating Hartlepool United's 2005 appearance in the League 1 play-off final.*

# *Forging Ahead with Graythorpe Forge*

Metal has fascinated men for millennia. The attraction of gold and silver is self-evident. But civilisation itself was forged first in the bronze age, and then in the iron age which followed.

Those who knew the secret of working with metal were respected members of the community. And they still are.

Industrial blacksmiths, steel fabricators and welders Graythorpe Forge and Engineering Ltd, based on the Graythorpe Industrial Estate, is one of the area's smaller firms, yet it is also one of the most well respected names.

CERTIFICATE OF APPROVAL

This is to certify that the Quality Management System of:

**Graythorpe Forge and Engineering Ltd**
**Hartlepool, Co. Durham**
**United Kingdom**

has been approved by Lloyd's Register Quality Assurance to the following Quality Management System Standards:

**ISO 9001:2000**

The Quality Management System is applicable to:

**Subcontract manufacture of pipeline supports, steel fabrications and forgings.**

Approval
Certificate No: LRQ 4004082

Original Approval: 2 October 2007
Current Certificate: 2 October 2007
Certificate Expiry: 1 October 2010

Issued by: Lloyd's Register Quality Assurance Limited

UKAS
001

This document is subject to the provision on the reverse
71 Fenchurch Street, London EC3M 4BS United Kingdom. Registration number 1879370

In 2004 the business was the subject of a management buy-out by an existing director and his wife, Gary and Joanne Attwood, following retirement of the previous owner.

Gary Attwood joined the business as an apprentice in 1982. He well recalls the work he did on HMS Warrior (now in Portsmouth) when the ship was in Hartlepool, before working his way up to become a company director.

Having already had 22 years of experience with the firm Gary knew the business inside out and had been running it for a number of years having worked his way up the company. With his knowledge and contacts setting up a family business seemed the next obvious step to take.

Following Gary and his wife Joanne's acquisition of the business in 2004 Joanne's role as director has been to manage IT and administration, utilising the skills she gained through her experience of running her own retail business for 13 years. In the years since then business has increased by a significant amount.

The Hartlepool company specialises in a range of engineering services including welding and fabrication, precision and general engineering and forging. The new owners quickly took on a new member of staff with plans to recruit a further five in subsequent years.

The Forge opened in 1968. The business has been based on the Graythorpe Industrial Estate site since 1979. Today the firm manufactures items such as structural steel work, pipe work, supports, special lifting equipment and stainless steel fabrications. Bespoke forgings, engineered parts and wrought iron work are carried out to customers' drawings or specifications.

Graythorpe Forge & Engineering Ltd has developed, documented and implemented a continuously improving Quality Management System based on the requirements of ISO 9001:2000. Today all processes are managed in accordance with ISO 9001:2000 requirements, whilst any outsourced processes that may affect product conformity will be controlled by means identified in the Quality Management System.

Today the strong directors team of Gary and Joanne are looking forward to growing the business even further by making their mark in new markets and capitalising on the unique facilities and skills of their business.

***Top left (facing page):*** *An ISO 9001:2000 Quality Management System Certificate awarded to Graythorpe Forge.* ***Far left (facing page) and top:*** *Views inside the works.* ***Above:*** *A selection of products manufactured by the company.*

# SHOPPING SPREE

Matthias Robinson extended his original Lynn Street drapery store to include rooms above to sell ladies' costumes and mantles. He gradually expanded into neighbouring premises when he acquired adjoining shops to create Manchester House. Robinson was an influential figure in West Hartlepool, serving on the first town council and acting as a Justice of the Peace. He became Mayor of Stockton in 1911. His golden rule in business was that employees should treat customers as they would wish to be treated themselves and the mantra served the company well. The store was so successful that the Coliseum, seen here in 1925, was built on the opposite side of the street and had furnishing departments, a café, offices, a carpet hall and model rooms. In 1912 a further addition to the empire was made when Birmingham House opened on nearby Whitby Street. By then, Robinson had expanded to include a major store in Stockton that opened in 1898. It was badly damaged in a fire a year later, costing the company thousands of pounds, but Robinson and son Arthur had a large, temporary wooden structure up and running as a replacement within a fortnight. Robinson's lost many staff and two of its directors on the battlefield during World War I, but it continued to thrive in peacetime. Another branch was opened in Leeds, but the Robinson name has now been swallowed by Debenham's.

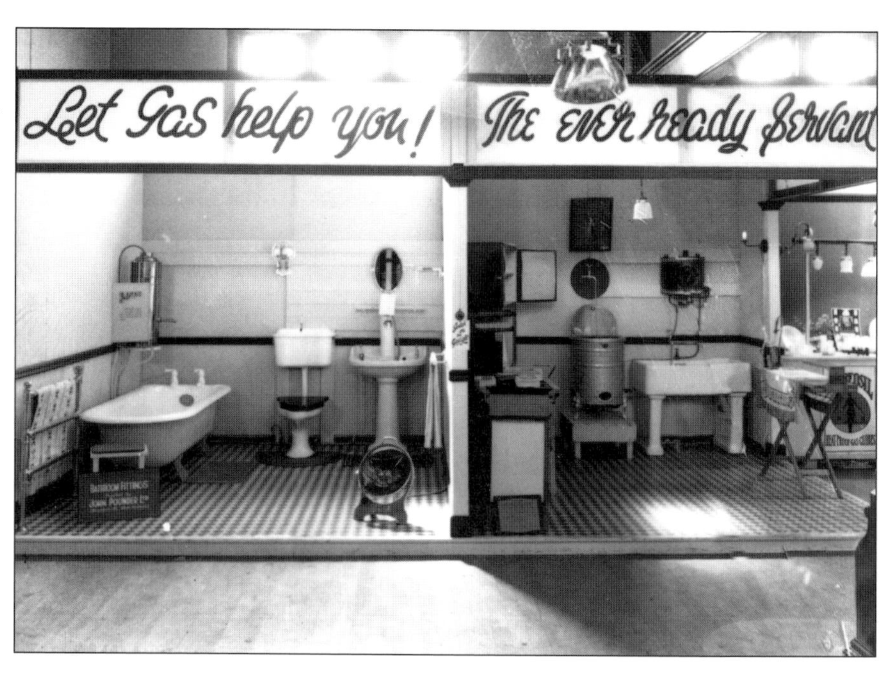


**Right:** In the early 1930s the Town Hall on Raby Street hosted an exhibition on behalf of the Gas Board. All manner of appliances from hot water boilers to fires and from cookers to fridges were on display. We can see from these tableaux the type of fittings that were once considered luxury items in our homes. The 1948 Gas Act nationalised the various individual gas companies into 12 area boards under the umbrella of British Gas. For over a hundred years prior to then gas had been manufactured and supplied by a series of private and municipally operated businesses. In 1966 the decision was taken to convert Britain to natural gas and a year later the first North Sea gas was brought ashore at the Easington Terminal. During a 10-year national conversion programme every appliance in the country was converted from town gas to run on natural gas. The use of gas in our homes goes back to William Murdoch, a Scottish engineer who moved to Redruth, Cornwall, in the late 18th century and was the first to install gas lighting in a house. The Valor gas cookers and Acme washers that we might recall from our parents' homes were developments from Murdoch's pioneering work. Which of us can forget the joy of getting a gas poker to use to light the fire, instead of that dreadful struggle with screwed up newspaper and sticks?

**Left:** The Emporium was West Hartlepool's Co-op, situated on the corner of Stockton Street and Park Road. It opened for business in 1915 on the site of a former school that had been built there in 1841. This shot shows how part of its interior looked in 1930. Shoppers will well remember the days when they went to the Co-op and collected stamps as part of the 'divvy' that could be cashed in when a fully stamped card was achieved. This all dated back to the group of businessmen and merchants on Toad Lane, Rochdale who got together to form the first co-operative group in 1844. Known as the Rochdale Pioneers, they started a period of phenomenal co-operative growth, particularly across the north of England at first. Business was conducted based on the Pioneers' eight 'Rochdale rules' that included distributing a share of profits according to purchases. In 1863 the Co-operative Wholesale Society (CWS) took on this name that we know it by today. By the end of the next decade the CWS had branched out into insurance, banking and manufacture, an amazing advancement from such humble beginnings. The pictured Co-op no longer serves the public as it once did. After remaining empty for several years and falling into disrepair, plans were realised recently to turn the Grade II listed building into luxury apartments, thus preserving one of the town's loveliest old structures.

**Left:** This form of cash register was a common sight in shops in the 1920s and this basic design continued to be used for several decades. With its chunky push buttons and pull down handle that clanked or rang a tinkling sound as a purchase was recorded, a number of these old machines have appeared in recent years in auction houses and commanded a good price as collectable items. Anyone who enjoyed the humour of Ronnie Barker will instantly equate this cash register with the one in his corner shop in BBC TV's 'Open all hours'. The sight of the drawer that nearly took his fingers off every time he closed it still makes viewers chuckle when they see repeats of the show, even though they know what is coming. This shop assistant epitomised the change in women's fashion that took place in the decade after World War I. On the lead in to the war, most women still favoured ground length dresses and clothing that resembled body armour in its thickness and cumbersome lack of manoeuvrability. A shortage of fabric during the war and a new sense of freedom inspired by the suffragette era liberated women from the costume confines of the early 1900s. More sombre designs were out as the bright young things of the 1920s drank, smoked and cut their hair short. Hemlines were raised and women's aspirations were lifted accordingly.

**Above:** Scott and Company was a firm of London tailors whose shop was on the corner of Lynn Street with Church Street. In 1925, boys as well as men were usually dressed in suits and natty flat caps, though many could only admire the quality of the tailoring on display in the shop window as these were times when money was tight. The immediate postwar years following the 1914-18 conflict saw Britain struggling to rebuild an economy that had been severely dented by the excesses of war. The cost to the nation had also been severe in terms of the loss of so many of its young men in the trenches of the Somme, Passchendaele, Ypres and the like, but those who survived still had to rebuild their lives in a world in recession. Wages were low and high employment was becoming increasingly difficult to maintain. Yet, there was still a level of pride to be maintained and the male population did its best. Quite often men had two suits to wear and they had to last. The first was for everyday use, while the second was just for best. It would be mothballed and reserved for weddings, funerals and special occasions, though the God fearing members of the community might deign to get it out of the wardrobe on Sundays.

**Top right:** The shop on Lynn Street pointed out that admission was free. That some establishments might charge a shopper for entering the premises seems a little bizarre to us in this day and age, but we still have some stores who follow a similar policy even now in that they charge you to park your car, though this is refunded if you make a purchase. Actively discouraging browsing still appears petty minded, even so. These 1930 shop girls, though, were keen to welcome you into their place of employment. Although not particularly well paid, a job here was a cut above one on the factory floor. Girls had to be articulate and numerate if they wanted to work behind the counter and it was certainly a more attractive position than a dirty, backbreaking manual role. Inter-war England witnessed the emergence of a new generation of socially and financially independent young working class women who gained jobs in offices and shops.

Mothers developed keen aspirations for their daughters, shaping the emergence of youth as a life stage marked by a degree of personal independence born of experiences of the Suffragette era. The famous St Michael brand name on some of the goods sold here had only been introduced in 1928 and the company was still strongly pushing its hardware lines, as well as the clothing it sold. Food departments were not added until later in the decade.

**Right:** Lynn Street was once the shopping centre of West Hartlepool. There is virtually nothing left now of the days when housewives flocked to the variety of shops and emporia that flourished here. Marks & Spencer was just one of the famous names that held a prime position on the street. Times change, fads come in and out of fashion, but some firms have become an institution and M&S, as everyone knows it, has become one of the fixtures on just about every high street in the country. In 1925 the company was still making its mark, if the reader will forgive the pun. It was back in 1884 that Michael Marks, a Russian-born Polish refugee, opened his first penny bazaar in Leeds Market. Next to the stall was a large poster proclaiming 'Don't ask the price, it's a penny'. Over the next few years Marks opened similar penny stalls in covered market halls all over Yorkshire and Lancashire. He formed a partnership with Tom Spencer, a warehouse cashier, in 1894. Marks continued to oversee the stalls and shops that they were opening at a rapid rate, while Spencer ran the office and warehouse for the expanding business. By 1907, both founders were dead and a new generation took the company forward. During the years between the two world wars, the company's expansion was rapid and M&S became a household name.

**Below:** Ever Ready became a household name in Britain in the 20th century. The country was slow to electrify and in the early years of the 1900s many rural areas had to do without electricity. There was a large battery market and huge numbers of radio batteries were sold, especially after the BBC went on air in the 1920s. By 1934 the sales of high tension radio batteries exceeded 15 million. Ever Ready was the leading name, but its origins were outside these shores. Akiba Horowitz, a Russian Jew, emigrated to the United States in 1891. He Americanised his name to Conrad Hubert and tried his hand at several jobs. He eventually found himself working for a company that made electrically illuminated novelty tie and scarf pins. He founded his own company and began producing battery operated cycle lights and torches under the Ever Ready name in the late 1890s. It became the market leader in Britain when it bought out the successful Lissen Company and took over its radio component factories. This photograph of a display of Ever Ready products will bring back to mind the days when today's 60-year-olds listened to Radio Caroline and the pirate DJs out at sea as they snuggled under the bedclothes with their trannies up to their ears.

**Right:** Every town had its own particular department store of quality that is now fondly remembered by older generations of shoppers. In more recent years these names have largely disappeared from our streets as the giants such as House of Fraser etc moved in and took them over. Family businesses just could not cope with the aggressive share dealing assaults or competition from such powerful monoliths. It was the same story all over the country and some capitulated by selling out while others just went to the wall. Bradford had its Busby's, Manchester its Paulden's and Sunderland its Binns', but they all lost their independence and, in some cases their existence, as big became beautiful, at least in financial terms. In our case it was Robinson's that felt the pinch. Lynn Street was graced with fine stores that boasted the Robinson name and it became synonymous with quality shopping. It was a sheer delight just to walk through the various departments and enjoy the variety of goods and services on offer. You could take tea and watch the world go by or just watch fascinated as canisters containing cash and orders whizzed across on high, powered by compressed air, as they winged their way from counter to cashier and back again. Manchester House, seen in 1930, on Lynn Street had developed from the little drapery shop that Matthias Robinson opened in 1875.

The House of Quality
CORSETS
BELTS

**Above:** It is recorded that Birmingham House was built in 1912, though the relief work on the building had the year 1913 upon it. It was part of the Robinson empire of department stores that reigned supreme in West Hartlepool for the best part of a century until Debenham's took them over in 1964. Several outlets were then demolished during the town centre redevelopment programme of the late 60s and early 70s. Standing on the corner of Whitby Street and Musgrave Street in the mid 1920s, Birmingham House was in the heart of West Hartlepool's main shopping area. This section, along with Lynn Street and Church Street, provided more than enough retail outlets to satisfy the needs of the town's population. There was refreshment to be had at the Shades Hotel, clothing to be cleaned at Johnson Brothers, sweets at Sample's, potions at Taylor's drugstore, balls to be potted at the billiard rooms and any manner of food, furniture, clothing and other goods to be purchased in shops both large and small. This part of the town was the town, in its retail sense. The developers ripped out its heart and tossed it aside when they built Middleton Grange. The horrid, brutalist style of concrete architecture, so common in new shopping centres and office blocks of that period, became our new retail mammoth. Thankfully, most of the interior was improved in 1993, but the likes of Birmingham House were long gone by then.

**Below:** The Health and Safety officials or the inspectors from Food Hygiene would have a fit if they came down Durham Street today and saw this display of meat hanging over the shop doorway. In 1910 it was usual to see hams, bacon, rabbits and other meats suspended from hooks outside a butcher's or general provisions store. E Billsborrow's general grocery shop had everything from apples at twopence a pound (that is 1p for 450 grams in newspeak) and butter at 1s 2d (6p) to best bacon, cocoa and meat extract. Billsborrow was not just a family grocer as he also provided provisions for the many ships based at the docks or that called there. Some of the brand names in this late Edwardian window are still very familiar today. Most of us will not recall Keenora, but Rowntree's and Oxo still occupy places on the shelves of every 21st century kitchen cupboard. The chocolate and cocoa firm was a thoroughly English company, being founded in 1862 by Henry Isaac Rowntree in York. Oxo, though, developed from a process developed by the German Julius Liebig in the 1840s. He was able to produce a concentrated beef extract to provide a substitute for the real thing for those unable to afford it. It was of liquid format and in a glass bottle. Liebig's Extract was rebranded as Oxo in 1899 and the first little cubes were manufactured about the time of this photograph.

**Left:** Every major retail chain had an outlet on Lynn Street in 1930. FW Woolworth's famous five and ten cent stores in America were translated into threepenny and sixpenny ones over here. Cheap and cheerful was the unwritten motto when the first outlet opened in Liverpool in November 1909. This was considered to be such a noteworthy occasion that the shop opened purely to allow potential customers to view the items that would be offered for sale. The store did not sell anything until 24 hours later. Frank Winfield Woolworth was a farm boy who became a shop assistant in New York. In 1879 he persuaded his employer to back him in opening his own place. His concentration on opening outlets in town centres, rather than on side streets, paid off. In Britain, there was rapid expansion after the Great War. The man in the street had little money to spare, so the keen prices at Woolworth's attracted his custom. The company increased its range of goods, introducing gramophone records, Ladybird clothing, a greater range of toys and games and a bigger selection of household items. As years went by, prices had to be upped from the original pair of amounts, but the concentration on value for money continued. However, this did not help some of the shopgirls who irritated customers by always asking 'How much is it love?' when they brought their purchases to the till.

# ACKNOWLEDGMENTS

*The publishers would like to sincerely thank the following individuals and organisations for their help and contribution to this publication*

*The staff at Hartlepool Central Library*

*David Hunter and the 500 Group (www.500group.org.uk)*

*Beamish Museum*

*Mr George Colley*